on your birthday,

July 11, 1960

from Phyllis
with love.

ENGLISH CHURCH DESIGN,
1040–1540 A.D.

The "British Heritage" Series
Uniform with this Volume

ENGLISH CHURCH CRAFTSMANSHIP
By F. H. CROSSLEY

PREHISTORIC ENGLAND
By GRAHAME CLARK

THE CATHEDRALS OF ENGLAND
By HARRY BATSFORD and CHARLES FRY

THE GREATER ENGLISH CHURCH
By HARRY BATSFORD and CHARLES FRY

THE PARISH CHURCHES OF ENGLAND
By J. CHARLES COX and C. BRADLEY FORD

THE ENGLISH ABBEY
By F. H. CROSSLEY

THE ENGLISH CASTLE
By HUGH BRAUN

THE ENGLISH GARDEN
By RALPH DUTTON

THE ENGLISH COUNTRY HOUSE
By RALPH DUTTON

THE ENGLISH COTTAGE
By HARRY BATSFORD and CHARLES FRY

ENGLISH VILLAGES AND HAMLETS
By HUMPHREY PAKINGTON

ENGLISH VILLAGE HOMES
By SYDNEY R. JONES

THE OLD TOWNS OF ENGLAND
By CLIVE ROUSE

THE OLD INNS OF ENGLAND
By A. E. RICHARDSON

THE OLD PUBLIC SCHOOLS OF ENGLAND
By JOHN RODGERS

THE HEART OF ENGLAND
By IVOR BROWN

THE COUNTRYMAN'S ENGLAND
By DOROTHY HARTLEY

OLD ENGLISH HOUSEHOLD LIFE
By GERTRUDE JEKYLL and SYDNEY R. JONES

OLD ENGLISH CUSTOMS AND CEREMONIES
By F. DRAKE-CARNELL

THE SEAS AND SHORES OF ENGLAND
By EDMUND VALE

THE SPIRIT OF LONDON
By PAUL COHEN-PORTHEIM

THE FACE OF SCOTLAND
By HARRY BATSFORD and CHARLES FRY

THE HEART OF SCOTLAND
By GEORGE BLAKE

THE LAND OF WALES
By EILUNED and PETER LEWIS

THE SPIRIT OF IRELAND
By LYNN DOYLE

BRITISH HILLS AND MOUNTAINS
By BELL, BOZMAN, etc.

Published by
B. T. BATSFORD LTD.
London · New York · Toronto
Sydney

1. THE TOWER OF DUNDRY CHURCH, SOMERSET

From a watercolour by John Chessel Buckler, 1827, in the Art Gallery, Bristol

English Church Design,
1040–1540 A.D.

A STUDY

by

FRED H. CROSSLEY, F.S.A.

Author of "The English Abbey," "English Church Craftsmanship,"
etc. etc.

Illustrated from

Drawings, Plans and Photographs

Second Edition, Revised and Enlarged

B. T. BATSFORD LTD

LONDON · NEW YORK · TORONTO · SYDNEY

First Printed, Summer 1945
Second Edition, Winter 1947–8

Books by the same author
in this series

THE ENGLISH ABBEY
ENGLISH CHURCH CRAFTSMANSHIP

MADE AND PRINTED IN GREAT BRITAIN BY
UNWIN BROTHERS LTD., LONDON AND WOKING
FOR THE PUBLISHERS, B. T. BATSFORD, LTD.
LONDON: 15 NORTH AUDLEY STREET, W.I
AND MALVERN WELLS, WORCESTERSHIRE
NEW YORK: 122 EAST 55TH STREET
TORONTO: 480–6 UNIVERSITY AVENUE
SYDNEY: 156 CASTLEREAGH STREET

PREFACE

A FEW readers may incline to the belief that I am a descendant of Don Quixote, a tilter at windmills; be that as it may, a revaluation of English mediaeval architecture is long overdue. Its gradual development met with the unqualified approval of the Victorian critics, who waxed enthusiastic over its details. However, in regard to the characteristic native developments later, when it ceased aping foreign schools and became definitely English, these quidhuncs solemnly announced that it had become debased. Not until the Black Death did it become a national style, owing but little to other countries, a functional architecture in complete harmony with the requirements of the time, sensible and beautiful, a product of the English compromise without exaggeration or foibles. It is unfortunate that it has suffered from the stupidities and indignities of the Victorians, who invariably preferred theory to fact, and who conferred upon it an entirely false set of values which have continued uncontradicted for nearly a hundred years. The object of this small book is to refute many of these statements and to endeavour to fit their dry bones into the cavalcade of time, finding a meaning in what these people called the styles, and a continuity of thought through the whole period.

FRED H. CROSSLEY

19 SHAVINGTON AVENUE, CHESTER
1945

PREFACE TO THE SECOND EDITION

ALREADY a new edition of this work has been called for, wherein numerous mistakes in the text have been amended. It has six additional full-page illustrations with an entirely new index.

The writer never intended the volume to be an elementary text-book, but a study of the essential continuity of English mediaeval architecture. Certain reviews have suggested that the book should be prefaced with a chapter on the general features and styles exhibited in a church. The author, however, has taken for granted that his readers already possess a modicum of understanding of the subject discussed.

CHESTER, 1947

v

ACKNOWLEDGMENT

WE are fortunate in obtaining permission, kindly given by Mrs. Griggs, to reproduce the late F. L. Griggs' etching of "The Potter's Bow." This, one of his finest imaginative etchings, displays his delicacy of vision into the spirit guiding the architectural output of the fifteenth century ; an insight almost without precedent. His early death was a grievous blow to those interested in etching, and in the meaning behind mediaeval building, regarding which it might be said that he was a prophet in retrospect. The Board of Education must be thanked for photographing the etching in exile.

Author and publishers are indebted for permission to reproduce drawings, photographs, etc., in the following quarters :—

Sir John Murray and the Executors of the late Professor Baldwin Brown for the plan of Brixworth Church ; Bristol Corporation Museum and Art Gallery Committee, through Dr. F. S. Wallis, Deputy and Acting Director, for the West View of Dundry Tower by John C. Buckler (frontispiece) ; Mr. J. Hervey Rutherford, F.R.I.B.A., for the drawing of Beverley Minster Towers ; Mr. Sydney Clough, F.R.I.B.A., A.R.C.A.(ARCH.)LOND. for the drawing of Hedon Tower.

With regard to the photographs, we have to thank Mr. Cecil Farthing (Conway Librarian of the Courtauld Institute), of the National Buildings Record, who has been extremely kind and helpful in obtaining photographic prints under difficult conditions. The majority of the subjects illustrated are from photographs taken by the author, and most of the remainder from views taken by the late Brian C. Clayton :— Figs. 12, 13, 14, 16, 17, 18, 19, 20, 25, 28, 31, 32, 49, 62, 63, 64, 82, 83, 88. 107, and 108. Thanks are also due to Mr. Herbert Felton, F.R.P.S. for Figs. 122, 124, and 126, Messrs. Frith of Reigate for Figs. 24 and 55, Mrs. Howard for permission to reproduce Figs. 53 and 73, taken by the late F. E. Howard, Mr. A. F. Kersting for Fig. 125 and Mr. Will. F. Taylor, Reigate, for Figs. 42, 120 and 123. Some photographs are from the Publishers' collection.

DEDICATION

TO THE MEMORY OF JOHN BILSON,
D.LITT., F.S.A.,

DOYEN OF MEDIAEVAL ANTIQUARIES,
THIS BOOK IS HUMBLY DEDICATED
BY A LIFE-LONG ADMIRER

CONTENTS

2 THE POTTER'S BOW

From an Etching by F. L. Griggs, R.A.

ENGLISH CHURCH DESIGN,
1040–1540 A.D.

SECTION I

AN INTRODUCTION AND A WARNING

"Restoration was a part of the Germanizing of Victorian England. The churches were made neat, tidy and soulless on a Teutonic pattern of Gothic. Lovely detail was ruthlessly destroyed in the process. The arch-restorer was Sir Gilbert Scott."

WILLIAM GAUNT, *The Pre-Raphaelite Tragedy*, page 188

THE rough and tumble fight for material supremacy in the sixteenth century destroyed the delicate spirit which guided the structure of mediaeval architecture and craftsmanship. This once gone was beyond recall, for its vision, provenance, and the reasons for its existence disappeared with it. Other forms of architectural inspiration might take its place and did, but they bore no relationship whatever to the architecture produced between 1150 and 1550.

In the nineteenth century, however, appeared what has been designated "the Gothic Revival," and under its banner dozens of churches were designed and erected conforming to the Victorian tenets of mediaeval architecture; a slavish copy of externals worked into the systematized course of correct rules and procedure; they composed a series of husks and shells masking the absence of the kernel within. The mediaeval period covering 400 years was divided by them into a number of definite styles in imitation of the classic mode, the earlier the style in date the more it was admired; these cut and dried sections became the models for many well known architects; Street chose to work in "The Early English Style"; Temple Moore in the "Decorated Style"; Pearson however went one better, for at Truro he invented a progressive style to cover the supposed length of time taken in the erection of his cathedral, a clever imitation of mediaeval procedure which has as little to do with serious architecture as a reconstruction of the tower of Babel. These styles were sufficiently trite when applied to the erection of churches, but became absurd when applied to secular buildings such as the Law Courts by Street founded upon Salisbury, or the design for Government buildings in Whitehall by Sir Gilbert Scott, which when turned down was used for the erection of the station hotel at St. Pancras.

I

B

The Tractarian movement propagated the fetish that the only correct place in which to worship God was in a "gothic" building, attempting thereby to bridge an impassable gulf between that of the essence of fifteenth century worship and its nineteenth century imitation. The chimerical resurrection of the spirit of mediaeval architecture was as hopeless as was that of Greece; both types of cultured and progressive building owe their delicacy and charm to the complexion of their times; in both instances they were homogeneous and self-contained.

In a study of our period we are placed at some disadvantage, for the output of four centuries suffered first severe destruction, followed by a period of neglect, and finally by drastic "restoration," not repair, so much so indeed that but few buildings remaining can be considered either mediaeval or genuine. What we usually find is a nineteenth century re-construction made to fit into Victorian theories; restorers had no compunction whatever in pulling down or cutting away anything which interfered with their conceptions of "gothic," or of which they failed to understand the meaning. The true evolution of mediaeval architecture escaped their vigilance; that the seeds of the fifteenth century style were inherent from the beginning never entered their heads; their interest in its development declined with the decrease of its growing pains, and curiously they had nothing but hard words for the *fait accompli*. Hardly a major building stands untransformed or has not been tinkered up to meet the notions of the time; a replacement of fifteenth century work by imitations from earlier styles fell in well with this scheme. In the Lady chapel at Chester lancets have taken the place of fifteenth century windows; the east end of the quire at Oxford now exhibits a terrible example of imitative twelfth century mannerisms. The Grimthorped transepts at St. Albans, though a tragedy, have their amusing side, for they are a ludicrous travesty of the real thing. Likewise the east end of Worcester and the west end of Nantwich are as false as Jezebel. It would indeed be difficult to find a finer set of examples illustrating the proverb that "the way to hell is paved with good intentions." At the present day this Victorian bastard "gothic" is completely in disrepute; it has unhappily effectually destroyed any taste for the real thing.

Modern architects tell us that they are only interested in "functional architecture"—whatever that may mean (?), for all architecture is and has been functional from the first or it is not architecture. If the mediaeval buildings blitzed during this recent war are ever repaired, the difficulty will be to find a

3 DURHAM CATHEDRAL, FROM THE SOUTH-WEST

4 GAWSWORTH CHURCH, CHESHIRE, FROM THE NORTH-EAST

modern architect who would care for the work, or be capable of carrying it out. We may however be spared another period of base imitation, for a mediaeval building is better patched than falsified.

An antiquarian point of view is necessary in our approach to the study of mediaeval architecture, treating it not as a living art which it ceased to be 400 years ago, but as a manifestation of the spirit of its time. With the growing knowledge of the period in which it flourished, noting the reasons influencing its development and the methods employed in its evolution, it will be possible to find a basis for study. Although we are now deprived of many reliable details, there are sufficient broad outlines remaining to form a fairly accurate picture of its progression. It is essential however to unlearn most of the text-book stuff written in the nineteenth century and to start with an open mind, cutting out the water-tight compartments of styles and realizing that mouldings and carvings are extraneous to the main progress of building.

That originally, mediaeval architecture was the least shackled of all architectural styles, less beset by rules and regulations, is now perhaps difficult to realize, for the nineteenth century has overlaid it with its theories and practice, especially the last; imitators invariably de-vitalize the spirit and accentuate the defects of what they copy. It certainly had defects which were inherent in its nature, and which militated against its eventual perfection, for the system of stress and strain carried with it the seeds of ultimate decay. Other styles had avoided this constant struggle to maintain stability; they were either earth-bound, built of uprights and horizontals as in the Greek and Egyptian styles, or they were well supported by huge blocks of masonry as in Roman and Byzantine building. It was only during the mediaeval time that the attempt was made to reach up to incredible heights held in position by stone scaffolding. The style was far in advance of the materials to hand, but not to the people, who were capable of amazing feats of daring; perhaps the result of inadequate knowledge or blind folly, but not lacking in imagination; an age of ceaseless experiment and restless development, with but little respect for the earlier stepping stones passed by the way.

Although from 1150 to 1550 this architecture was gradually transmuted by reason of fresh requirements and artistic considerations, during the whole of the time we hear little of professional architects; master-masons yes, men who through ability rose to the head of their profession by their creative genius, and of whom but little is known; we however know more of the men who ordered and financed the works and who took to themselves the praise; Alan of Walsingham; William of Edington; and William of Wykeham. Professional architects came into prominence only with the decline of the national style, and with their advent architecture became an individualistic thing according to the whims and fancies of fashion. A taste for Egyptian, Greek, Byzantine, Roman, Tudor, French, German or Italian could be indulged in at will; but the accumulated knowledge of the world's styles precluded the possibility of the fruition of any national style.

In the beginning of the era it was a question of re-learning the arts of building afresh, for the destructive and bestial habits of uncontrolled mankind had once more left little to go upon, and that little misunderstood. After the Norman invasion however the urge to build gradually took possession of the race, a sure sign of returning sanity and civilization; time and labour were freely expended for several decades in the difficult task of re-learning, for everything had to be first tried out, and proficiency gained was only through bitter disappointments and disaster. A method of building having been first grasped, the foundations were laid for what was to follow. When the country had settled down after a period of rapine and bloodshed it devoted itself to the things that mattered, and the inertia of the first fifty years disappeared. Walls were more carefully laid, constructed with finer joints, less rubble was used and less weight of material employed, and the art of building advanced.

After this prelude of Romanesque building at a date somewhere about 1150, the main characteristic of mediaeval architecture was developed in the constructional use of the pointed arch. This released the masons from the constrictions imposed upon them by the semicircular arch, and gave to them a freedom undreamt of before. So great was this liberation, that construction quickly soared in attenuated and slender buildings. With the monastic revival brought about by the Cistercian Order, full use was made of this new architecture; these high gabled, narrow windowed, well buttressed buildings are typical of the monastic ideal in its aloofness and austerity. The third quarter of the thirteenth century found secular bishops, regal princelings and nobles much in evidence, which was again reflected in the architecture of the day. The churches, though perhaps less in height, were broadened out and became more ornate. From 1250 to 1330 decoration was used in profusion, the earlier trefoil blossoming into natural foliage, which again became later crystallized into a bulbous variety. This gorgeous pageant of chivalry, colour and decoration was abruptly closed by the Black Death.

From 1350 to 1550 the parish church took the premier position. The scourge had depleted the monasteries, and combined with the wars of the Roses decimated the aristocracy. The plague turned the thoughts of the people toward serious things, and the popularity of prayers for the dead focussed attention upon their own parish churches. The rich merchants, many of whom now occupied the position formerly held by the nobles, showed considerably more interest in the churches of their districts than in either the aloof convent or the self-centred cathedral; they spent both time and money in rebuildings and enlargements; therefore the architecture of the last two-hundred years, which had become a truly national style, is best reflected and may best be studied in the parish churches, especially those on the east coast and in the south-west.

With the Reformation, however, mediaeval architecture ceased as a living force, and for the next 300 years became a word of reproach. The very name "gothic" was given it in contempt; it signified all that was barbarous, rude and unshapely, and so it must have appeared to the "enlightened" eighteenth century folk, for they had little use for it except as a picturesque ruin or for constructing a garden grotto. They lived in a world of elegance and artificiality, bemused by the discussions of logicians and philosophers.

During the 400 years the evolution of architectural design was fairly constant and at times rapid, but was unequal in its distribution. Those parts of the country furthest from the centres of progress lagged behind sometimes as much as fifty years. From the commencement dissimilarities of detail are to be observed; the attenuated lancet windows found in the thirteenth century work in Northumbria, and the fourteenth century florid Yorkshire school are instances of this. Differences in planning and construction were governed by the abundance or lack of good building stone more than by the question of finance or available labour. Should the stone near the site be poor, what was the chance of transport by water; these considerations produced many local types and variations from the norm. During the last phase the national style developed further individualities of form and design which would make an interesting and agreeable study of itself.

In examining a church at the present day, the outside has little genuine carving and window tracery to show; 400 years of weather, rain, snow and frost have taken their toll of the work of both masons and carvers; the industrial expansion of the nineteenth century however was more effective and thorough in its destruction, with its pall of soot and chemical fumes corroding and disintegrating the quality of even the hardest stones. The west porch at Ely and the north porch at St. Mary Redcliff are modern reproductions as far as could be ascertained from the decayed and rotting fragments that remained. The interiors suffered in another form, first from their adaptation through the centuries to the bigotries of religious factions, losing interest and genuineness in the process. Whitewash had multiplied and many coats encrusted the walls and carvings, actually preserving them from decay; however, the rough and thorough methods employed in chiselling, scraping and cutting away this accumulation of preservative destroyed what it had preserved, not only the carvings but the wall paintings, which were sacrificed wholesale to the lust for naked walls and the puritan horror of beauty, for although the fashionable urge was to restore a church, it was usually controlled by certain tenets of dogma; as a parson of Gawsworth, Cheshire, wrote in 1852,

"while the essential objects of a Protestant church have been especially kept in view, there has been no needless sacrifice of architectural propriety. Every feature of antiquity not inconsistent with our purified religion has been carefully preserved."

This quotation gives to us a guide as to the attitude of the clergy to restoration in addition to that of his architect.

Not that repair was unnecessary, far from it; the neglect of centuries had spelt disaster; gutter and leaking roofs neglected, galleries erected with no regard for the building or its safety; more serious however was the manner in which for monetary gain the interiors of the churches were turned into charnel houses, the foundations of piers and walls sapped and undermined within, while buttresses and supports decayed without. This custom is aptly put on a gravestone at Kingsbridge, Devon,

"Here I lie at the chancel door, Here I lie because I'm poor,
The further in the more you pay, but here I lie as happy as they."

It is however one thing to repair and another thing to restore, for they are the antithesis of each other. Restoration means the replacing of what the fond architect imagined to have disappeared and putting the architectural clock well back; repair is preserving only what exists, a most difficult thing to do when a man suffers from itching fingers.

In addition to the falsifying of the construction there are other snags and pitfalls lying in wait for the serious student. Appearances are often made deceptive by cunning and artifice.

5 GLOUCESTER CENTRAL TOWER, FIFTEENTH CENTURY

6 ST. MARY REDCLIFF, SOUTH CLERESTORY OF NAVE

While Selby Abbey was a-restoring from the devastating fire, I stood upon the walls of the new central tower and remarked to the carver, "but surely, the splendid fourteenth century pinnacles of the quire perished in the heat, and yet, there they are smoke blackened but not much the worse"; said my friend, "they perished all right, what you see is my work, smoke blackening as well." This same clever carver was employed in his spare time recutting the carving upon the wall arcades of the nave aisles at Beverley Minster, and at times, owing to his careful treatment of both mediaeval and modern it is difficult at a first glance to tell which is the genuine and which the fake.

Another pernicious habit is the foul re-chiselling of the walls, especially within the church, sometimes occasioned by stripping the plaster, whether mediaeval or modern, irrespective as to whether the walling is ashlar or rubble. Mediaeval practice was from the first to cover the walls with a thin coat of plaster; its demolition is both unintelligent and perverse, causing many churches to look little better than barns. Unfortunately it is still practised, for within the last ten years Wrenbury in Cheshire has suffered the same ignominy, left stripped and naked.

In an examination of a building it is well to take nothing upon trust. When possible, a drawing, photograph or engraving taken before the restoration should be studied; this may sometimes be found in the vestry (should the door be found unlocked), it will point the way in discovering the malpractices of the restorer. With regard to Gyffylliog in the Vale of Clwyd, Archdeacon Thomas tells us that it was carefully restored in 1876 under the care of Mr. Arthur Baker. What actually took place was the removal of the roofs, replaced by a different type with very thin scantling; the renewal of all the windows in a different stone and to a fresh pattern; the destruction of the south doorway and porch, using the west end as an entrance; the abolition of the mediaeval screen and the eighteenth century west gallery with the use of the carved detail to decorate the new clumsy choir fittings and chancel roof; finally, as it was originally an undivided church, the architect has placed an oak arch between the nave and the chancel. It is to all purposes a new church erected upon old foundations, and for this wanton and senseless destruction the architect is congratulated for a piece of careful restoration by a church dignitary with antiquarian leanings.

The repair of a mediaeval church should be entrusted to the hands of antiquarian experts, certainly not handed over to a general practitioner, possibly "suffering from enlarged perceptions," and not content with repair. Men who have devoted their lives to the study of their subject are more likely to do

justice to it than a man unversed in an exacting piece of work.
A fine example of this procedure is the work of the late G. McN.
Rushforth, M.A., F.S.A., who undertook the repair of the
mediaeval glass at Malvern Priory and Tewkesbury Abbey,
and by deduction and expert knowledge brought the work to a
triumphal conclusion.

7 DURHAM CATHEDRAL, THE GALILEE. 1175

8 BEVERLEY MINSTER, LOOKING EAST

ON THE DESIGNING OF TOWERS

In taking a bird's-eye view of the towers of the parish churches of England and Wales one is at once struck, not only by their number but by their variety; they are a necessary complement to any church and parish which had either the ambition or the means to erect one, from the plain and humble to the magnificent, and from towers which in their early days had been used principally as dwellings or places of refuge and defence, to the later glorious examples which form the western portals to the churches which they adorn; nor must we forget their use as bell-houses, where from the seventeenth century onwards there sprang up rival bands of ringers, competing in the strenuous exercise of change ringing, filling the air with the clangorous noise from their brazen-throated monsters.

The differences shown in the design of towers, their position in the plan of churches and the materials used in their construction are more varied than one would suppose. In plan, towers may be square, oblong, round or oval, hexagonal and octagonal; and they may occupy positions at the crossing, the west end, the end of an aisle, placed against the side of the chancel, forming a transept, or entirely detached from the main fabric of the church as at West Walton and Ledbury, or connected by a passage as at Garway, Herefordshire. Towers are usually built of stone but other materials were employed such as brick, flints and timber. They have been erected continuously from pre-conquest times down to the present day, the latest, the stupendous central tower of the new cathedral at Liverpool, is over 300 feet in height and of sufficient girth to contain the Mersey tunnel within its walls.

In considering the beauty of a tower apart from its utility, it is surprising to find how seldom a tower, when carefully examined, fulfils the qualifications of perfection. In no other mediaeval building are there so many "ifs" and "buts" to our appreciation of the proportions and decoration. The west doorway too small, the window above too large, the middle storey too fussy, the belfry too plain; the buttresses wrongly placed, perhaps too small and skimpy, or omitted as at Manaton and Kingskerswell in Devon. The crown inadequate, the vice either omitted or in the wrong position; a too redundant use of horizontal strings breaking up the wall surface and apparently

9

shortening the height of the tower. The general proportions too massive for the height as at Cound, Salop, or too attenuated as at Bovey Tracey, Devon. Of how many towers may it be said that but for this or that it would be perfect!

It is well therefore before beginning the study of towers to consider a few guiding principles by which the finer towers may be judged and appreciated. Apart from the general proportion of width to height and its suitability to the fabric of the church, there are many details to be examined such as mouldings, strings, buttresses, windows, doorways and decoration generally, all of which play an essential part in either making or marring a design. A tower wall five feet from the ground is usually between four to five feet in thickness, as it ascends it should batter slightly, at least half an inch to every yard of the exterior. This gradually diminishes the weight of the wall, producing a strong vertical line at the same time. If the exterior walls are kept perfectly straight all the way up, the tower will appear to broaden out and look top-heavy. To the eye, tower walls should always be adequately buttressed, whether they really require the support or not; without this adjunct a tower looks poor if not unsafe, an excellent reason why many post-reformation towers are unsatisfactory in outline.

Buttresses may be clamp, diagonal or four-square, but in every case ought to be substantial. If built against each face of the tower they should not meet, but be set back sufficiently to allow the corners of the tower to be seen, thereby giving an added vertical line to the eye as at Ipplepen in Devon and Backwell and Chew Magna in Somerset; moreover they should reach the crown of the tower and finish in crocketed pinnacles, and not stop at some intermediate stage as they so frequently do. A fine feature of many towers especially in the south-west is an external vice, placed either in the centre of a face giving a strong line as at Wellington, Somerset, or at a corner completed by a spirelet and pinnacles as at Banwell and Ilminster, also in Somerset. The string courses, with the exception of a deeply moulded base course and the top string under the parapet, should not be so strongly accentuated as to break the upward sweep of the eye; it is indeed better for the strings to be confined to the west face. The vertical line was one that was not sufficiently entertained; when employed it is usually successful; there are differing ways of producing this effect either by blind tracery panelled upon the surface in the Severn Valley format found at Gloucester (5), Malvern, Worcester and Chipping Campden, or by the use of long narrow windows in the belfry stage shown at Cottingham, East Riding, Yorkshire, Oundle, Northampton-

9 ST. ALBANS, FROM AMBULATORY TO SOUTH AISLE

10 GLOUCESTER CATHEDRAL, SOUTH TRANSEPT INTO NAVE

shire, and St. Neots and Keyston, Huntingdonshire. Another form was to continue the belfry windows downwards by blind tracery as at Batcombe, Evercreech and St. Cuthbert's, Wells (13); this is still further accentuated at Wrington and Evercreech by a centre pinnacled shaft rising without a break through the two storeys completed above the battlements, flanked at Evercreech by similar shafts to the corners; in none of the examples cited are the lines broken by strong horizontal strings. The grouping of corner pinnacles in triplicate adds to this effect, St. Cuthbert's, Wells (13), being the one tower in which they are disproportionate. At Chipping Campden a better design would have been produced by taking the vertical lines down without a break, in place of restarting below a string with a fresh set of tracery heads. Campden is the one tower of this series in which the buttresses are set diagonally and not four-square or clamp.

On the west face, the doorway is usually too small for good proportions, as at Wells cathedral (12); this may be remedied in towers by panelled decoration if taken across the west face from buttress to buttress as at Crewkerne, Somerset, and Tarvin, Cheshire; or by the use of side niches as at Kingston St. Mary, or Wybunbury in Somerset and Cheshire. A well set-back window above the doorway gives an appearance of solidity and strength, its size kept in proportion to the doorway below it. The chief interest however is naturally the belfry stage, care being taken to ensure this feature by keeping the lower stages quite simple. The windows of the belfry may be either single or grouped, each complete in itself, or placed together under a single weather-moulding; the top stage may be designed as an arcade with real or blind tracery divided by shafted pinnacles; excellent examples of the triple arcade are on the towers at Witney, Oxfordshire, and Ketton, Rutland, in five at Oundle in the same county, four at King's Norton and three in many of the towers of Somerset, such as Banwell, Cheddar and Weare. Nichework may be placed in various positions, one either side the doorway, the second storey with three, or one either side the window, sometimes repeated on each face of the tower. Other decoration is applied, gargoyles from whose backs the pinnacles spring, bands of enrichment under the parapet or above the doorway designed with blind tracery either in trefoil or quatrefoil, groups of pinnacles placed upon the tops of buttresses as at Shepton Mallet, Somerset; continuously moulded battlements as on the towers of Cheshire, or the more openwork tracery used for parapets in Yorkshire, as at Beverley and Lincolnshire.

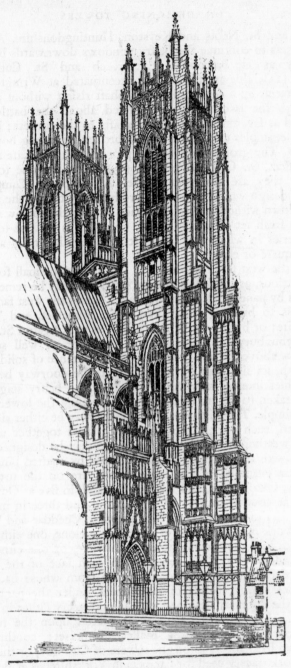

BEVERLEY MINSTER: THE WESTERN TOWERS
From a drawing by J. Hervey Rutherford, F.R.I.B.A.

Materials play an important part in the designing of towers. In Devon and Cornwall the granite and gritstone are of an uncompromising texture, resulting in towers which though a little grim and stark are effective in their quiet strength (24). In contrast, the towers of Somerset are built of freestones from Doulting and Dundry, to name but two quarries, stone easily worked providing the material for elaborations of which the master-masons were quick to take advantage, the country possessing as many excellent towers as the rest of England. In East Anglia flints bedded in plenty of mortar were used owing to the scarcity of freestones, the decoration was provided by thin layers of fretted stone contrasting with the split dark flints. The Nene valley oolites found material for a splendid series of spired towers of the thirteenth and fourteenth centuries. The magnesian limestone of Yorkshire allowed of careful and delicate handling, while the coarse red-sandstones of the west inhibited the mason from making any such attempts.

Coming from the general to the particular, we find that the enthusiasm of the wealthy merchants and wool-staplers of the fifteenth century provided the funds for many of the finest towers scattered over England, especially Somerset. There was no lack of stone or labour, furthermore the master-masons were rich in ideas, each man designing his own version of a perfect tower, with the result that the county is dotted over with lovely steeples, every group having its own individuality of style in the arrangement of the belfry windows, the setting out of the vice and buttressing, as in the parapeting which could be as simple as it could be splendid, the cornice bristling with pinnacles and spirelets forming the crown to the tower.

There have been several classifications of the eighty Somerset towers of note, the first by Professor Freeman, the second by R. P. Brereton and the third and latest by Dr. F. J. Allen, who has divided them into eight groups. The source of inspiration of this widespread building design may be traced to the cathedral towers at Wells (12), the central tower of fourteenth century date, the western towers 1386 and 1424 respectively, and, although many glorious versions were later evolved, the towers of Wells have never been surpassed; they are completely satisfying in their proportions, outline and design. Many of the earlier towers, as the central tower at Wells and the western tower at Shepton Mallet, were designed for stone spires which were never carried out. The towers in Somerset may be classed either by the number of belfry lights or by the setting out of the buttresses. A fair number of the single windowed type have the buttresses set within the wall space giving prominence to the corners of the towers appearing between them. In the two-windowed type the buttresses are more closely set, and the angles of the tower disappear at the belfry stage. (The diagonal buttress is an exception in this county.) The buttresses were terminated in several ways; at Ile Abbots (14) in crocketed shafts before reaching the cornice.[1] At Chew Magna and Winford the line is continued by a small shaft to the top of the parapet; at Norton St. Philip the buttresses have pinnacles rising above the parapet, at Hinton St. George they are combined with a corner pinnacle making three, and at Backwell with ornamental turrets. At Leigh-on-Mendip and Mells, prominence is given to the twin shafts which become detached towards the top and are placed before a corner pinnacle, while at Banwell, Batcombe, Bruton, Cheddar and many other towers the buttresses become diagonal half-way up the belfry stage. The crowns vary, the more elaborate have the major pinnacles surrounded by smaller ones, projecting pinnacles supported by flying buttresses at the corners, openwork battlements and turrets with bands of ornament, and at North Petherton the upper part of the tower is covered by reticulated tracery. At Bristol St. Stephen, Dundry (1) and Taunton St. Mary, the crowns are greatly enriched and the vices completed by spired roofs surrounded by pinnacles.

There is in this county a tendency to over-elaboration, especially on the intermediate stages of the towers where as at Batheaston, Chew Magna, Dundry, Portishead and several other examples, the single window is monotonously repeated in each four stages of the tower; when we come to the ornate tower of Taunton St. Mary we are confronted with a repeat of two windows to each ascending storey; this design is unfortunately aggravated by the deadly precision and dull mechanical accuracy employed when the tower was rebuilt in the nineteenth century.

Niches with spiring canopies are freely used, especially on either side of the windows of the second storey, sometimes repeated on all four sides as at Weston Zoyland. In the Banwell niches two figures remain illustrating the Annunciation, two pots of lilies growing from the cill of the window in between them. In a few towers weather mouldings above the windows have been omitted, such as Leigh-on-Mendip, Mells and Kingsbury Episcopi, but generally the over decoration of Somerset towers becomes an obsession and one is glad to find the plain north face of such a tower as West Pennard. Many of the towers

[1] Bishops Lydard, Huish Episcopi, Kingston St. Mary, North Petherton, Staple Fitzpaine and Taunton St. James.

11 BEVERLEY MINSTER, ENTRANCE TO CHAPTER HOUSE

A FINE EXAMPLE OF A GREAT WESTERN ICONOSTASIS SCREEN

12 WELLS CATHEDRAL. WEST FRONT

are quite tiny as at Weare and Publow, but remain proportionate in scale, delightful miniatures of greater examples.

In Devon a group of quite distinctive and closely related towers include Ashburton, Harberton, Little Hempston, Ipplepen and Tor Bryan (15) with Wellington just over the border into Somerset. Owing to the intractability of the material employed, the masons made a virtue of necessity and produced an imposing if rather bleak tower, solid, without ornament, rising sheer from base to crown, with the exception of a couple of strings, the vertical lines strongly emphasized by buttress and vice; this latter of octagonal form placed in the centre of a face, usually the south, and by planting the buttresses within the angles of the tower, cutting out all but two of the off-sets, giving a series of unbroken vertical lines leading the eye to the summit. The severity of design is enhanced by the smallness of the grouped belfry lights combined with slit-lights up the vice and the defensive character of the towers by the heavily battlemented parapets. The west doorway and windows are unaggressive and the middle storeys plain. Totnes is rather an exception to this group for it combines features from other types; however, the south side has its buttresses well brought in enclosing a vice between; the crown of the tower has large octagonal turrets with crocketed spires. This group demonstrates admirably how possible it is to build both finely proportioned and dignified towers when the ordinary forms of decoration and arrangements of the belfry are denied.

Across the Bristol channel in Pembrokeshire and in parts of Glamorganshire, is a series of towers of more simple form and severe outline; the majority without buttressing, string courses, important windows or doorways, rising undivided and clear with a slight batter to the machicolated parapets. The majority have a square turret vice at a corner, often over-topping the parapets as at Newport; at Haverfordwest however the turret is octagonal. The doorways are small and the towers are without the usual west window; the belfry lights are narrow slits, one, two or three, occasionally protected by a weather moulding. The vice has slit lights and the towers have every appearance of being originally built for defence; such towers as those at Begelly, Robeston West, Johnston and Loveston are reminiscent of the early days of sea pirates when a refuge was essential.

The towers of East Anglia provide a strong contrast to the Somerset type, for stone in this district of the eastern side of England is as scarce as it is plentiful in the west; other building material had therefore to be found, and flint pebbles bedded in mortar were plentifully used. This however precluded any lavish use of stone enrichments either niche or canopy; its place was taken by what is called "flushwork," a method of inlaying thin slabs of stone upon the surface of the walls producing an excellent contrast to the dark split flints; under the parapets a band of flushwork is often found combined with inlay on the parapets. Good examples of flushwork are to be found upon the towers at Earl Stonham, Eye, Ipswich St. Lawrence, Laxfield, Redenhall and Southwold (38). There are of course exceptions, for Laxfield is partly faced in stone, and in Norfolk near the Wash, stone was used because it could be transported by water. Swaffham is a noble example of fine proportions, with long three-light windows to the belfry stage which is completed by a splendid parapet; the lower half of the tower is quite plain, for the builders of this district knew the advantages of plain spacing. The average tower is substantial, fairly tall, plain and dignified with medium sized belfry windows which are single, with few exceptions, as at Eye, Mendlesham and Cromer, this last spoilt by the windows being set too low. Horizontal strings are inconspicuous and at Worlingworth the tower is without them. There is no general rule here with regard to the setting out of buttresses; Lavenham and Swaffham have well spaced four-squared type; Aylsham and Bramford the close type; Earl Stonham, Framlingham, Southwold (38) and Worlingworth diagonal buttressing, whereas Dedham, Bungay, Eye and Laxfield have octagonal buttresses completed by heavy turrets. Vices are rare and they seldom reach to the top of the tower excepting in the Essex districts; they finish either at the second storey as at Castle Acre, or at the belfry stage as at Bramford and Earl Stonham. The towers of East Anglia form a distinctive group and show in their design and construction both knowledge and care.

In the Yorkshire area, in which the numerous monastic establishments led the way to excellent masoncraft and design, the towers have a quality and character of their own, although perhaps they are not readily grouped. The Cistercian Order and the Augustinians between them gradually taught the masons an accomplished and thoroughly efficient system of masonry and building; this was aided by the quality of the lime and freestones quarried in the district resulting in well-proportioned towers, sound in judgment and free from excesses, for plainness had been a tenet of the Cistercians, the decoration being confined to the delicate and lacelike character of the open parapets placed upon such towers as Beeford, Holme, Tickhill and Thirsk, and in Nottinghamshire, where Yorkshire influence was strong at Blyth. Belfry windows were either single or in

14 ILE ABBOTS

13 WELLS, ST. CUTHBERT'S

BRICKWORK IN TOWER CONSTRUCTION
FIFTEENTH CENTURY

THE UNCOMPROMISING DEVON METHOD

pairs; of the first, Great Driffield is a noble example together with Blyth and Thornhill.[1] Examples of windows in pairs include central towers, at Cottingham, Hatfield, Hedon and Howden; western towers at Fishlake, Sprotborough and Tickhill. Buttresses in plan are divided between the close four-square type at Hatfield or the diagonal at Beeford, or the mixture of both at Hedon (p.18); they vary in height, some of them reaching to the parapet, or half-way down the belfry, or below it as at Sprotborough. Many Yorkshire off-sets are enriched with crocketed gables as at Hatfield, Hedon and Tickhill. Against the moorlands a sterner type of tower was built, as at Halifax, where the fine tall uncompromising smoke-blackened steeple stands amidst bleak hills, bold, strong and sturdy, and at Grinton (23), Swaledale, unadorned and severe.

In Wiltshire many towers have square-headed windows and panelling upon the belfry stage, a distinguished design enhanced by the plainness of the lower part of the tower illustrated at Nettleton, Yatton Keynell and Westwood, the last ennobled by a large octagonal vice, crowned by an ogee canopy of stone. Melksham has intriguing tracery, but as this tower has been transferred from a central to a western position, the genuineness of its detail may well be open to doubt. The central tower at Bath is related to this type but has heavy octagonal corner buttresses, whereas the Wiltshire towers have scant buttressing, excepting Nettleton. In Dorset, Charminster has double square-headed windows, with heavy buttressing of the four-square type and a good turret, otherwise Dorset tower design reflects the Somerset style.

A Midland type has the belfry stage arcaded; in four at King's Norton and Coleshill, in three at Bromsgrove. The same setting out is found at Northleach, Gloucester, but this county has a divided allegiance—the lower half influenced by Somerset in complete contrast to the simple dignity of Winchcombe—the upper half showing the Severn Valley format with such panelled towers as Malvern, Worcester and Gloucester (5) with St. Mary-le-Crypt in the same city, or the ugly freakish example at Cirencester.

It is impossible to describe a quarter of the splendid towers scattered over the country which belong to no particular group. Denbighshire possesses two fine towers at Wrexham and Gresford (22), the former of large girth, panelled, niched and pinnacled, the latter one of the loveliest ever built. The lower stage is of fourteenth century date, but the early sixteenth

[1] With lesser towers at Beeford, Eastringham, Holme-on-Spalding-Moor, Skipton and Bainton.

century belfry stage is an inspiration, faultless, and a fitting companion to the tower of Magdalen College, Oxford. Other

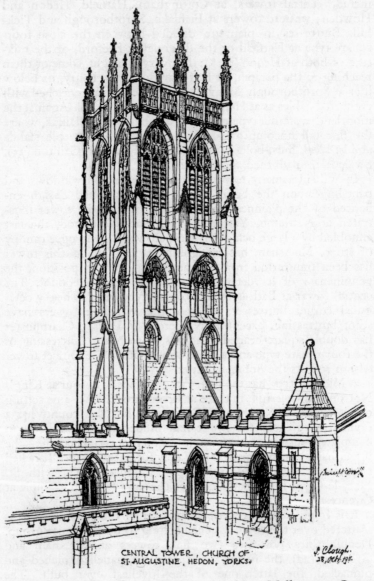

CENTRAL TOWER, CHURCH OF
ST. AUGUSTINE, HEDON, YORKS.

J. Clough.
28. Oct. 1911.

towers include St. Neots, Huntingdonshire; Melbourne, Cambridgeshire; Whissendine, Rutland; Cricklade, Wiltshire, and the charming tower at Shrawbury, Salop, this last akin to the

TENTH CENTURY IMITATIVE TIMBERWORK

CIRCULAR FLINT BUILT TOWER

18 HADDISCOE, NORFOLK, ED. THE CONFESSOR DATE

17 EARLS BARTON, NORTHAMPTONSHIRE

FOURTEENTH CENTURY SPIRE DESIGN, BROACH AND OTHERWISE

20 PICKWORTH, LINCOLNSHIRE

19 HIGHAM FERRERS, NORTHAMPTONSHIRE

towers of Cheshire. This small county has nevertheless an individual series of its own; the towers are nowhere large but are carefully designed, proportionate in mass and detail and pleasing to look at especially Gawsworth (4), Backford, Handley, Shotwick, Tattenhall and Weaverham.

With the exception of Wells (12) the greater church towers have remained unmentioned, for towers are relatively of greater importance to parish churches; it is to them that they look to show their position on the map. Greater churches however possess many magnificent central towers; never a very satisfactory form, judged from a constructional point of view, standing as they do upon four legs and having to rely upon subsidiary buildings both for abutment and upkeep. History tells of their precarious character, as, owing to faulty construction, insecure foundations and over weighty additions many of them fell, destroying much of the churches in the process. Various palliatives were tried out to prevent collapse; at Wells and Glastonbury inverted arches were used against all four legs, strong stone girder arches at Canterbury, side arches at Salisbury; stone pulpitums bolstered up others, which when removed by restoring architects was followed by collapse, as at Chichester. Arcades, triforiums and clerestories in proximity to the tower piers were built up, in fact many experiments were essayed but few were successful.

The majority of the towers as we see them today are the work of more than one century, as at Durham (3), Salisbury and Ripon; some have remained low as originally built at Winchester, Boxgrove and Peterborough, this last now rebuilt. Others are the efforts of a single period, especially that of the twelfth century shown at Castor, Norwich, St. Albans, Southwell and Tewkesbury; fourteenth century Hereford and the later Bristol, with fifteenth century Canterbury and Gloucester, together with the glories of the great lanterns at Lincoln and York. In comparing the methods of the varying periods we find a return in the last phase of the habits of the first, that of decorating the wall surface with ornament; in the first, the wall arcades of Castor and Tewkesbury are surface decoration, in the last however the sunk panelling applied to the towers of Gloucester (5) and Malvern are constructional; the panelling enabled the walls to be thinned down, the stone ribs acting as sinews to the framework.

Certain greater churches had a single tower at the west end in addition to a central one; these unfortunately were even less successful in keeping their equilibrium, for they usually enclosed the last bays of the nave in place of starting from their own

foundations. Both Hereford and Malmesbury collapsed, Shrews-
bury still stands, as does Ely, owing perhaps to the lateral
abutments of transepts. Other western towers were erected
when the naves became parochial as at Waltham, Wimborne
and Wymondham. For the west front of a great church, however, twin towers are the finest in design, and there are many
examples remaining in England of this magnificent treatment of
the western façade. A few examples are the result of nineteenth
century rebuilding as a tower at Canterbury, Llandaff and
Bridlington. The grouping of a central and two western towers
in a single building is an impressive architectural achievement,
especially when placed upon a dominating situation such as
Durham (3) or Lincoln. The three spires of Lichfield form a
charming group, and the mediaeval city of Coventry with its
three spires supplemented by many others must have presented
a scene hardly less lovely than was Oxford before the degrada-
tion of the modern industrial eruption.

Historically considered towers have a remote past, but for
English examples we need hark back no further than the
seventh century to find the beginnings of our subject. The
design, structure and position of towers are the results of the
traditions brought with our conquerors from other countries,
including Saxony, Denmark and the Norse lands. Celtic and
Italian missionaries who were the first to attempt the conversion
of this country to Christianity, superimposed their own ritual
arrangements upon this early foundation. The early stage was
set in Northumbria where Benedict Biscop in 674 and 681
founded his twin monasteries at Monkwearmouth and Jarrow;
the lower parts of both towers and the one at Corbridge were
originally the western porches connecting these churches to
their forecourts; it was not until a later date they received the
superstructure of towers. The same evolution took place at
Brixworth, Northamptonshire, but in this case as at Brigstock
a large semi-circular vice was placed in front. Another example
is the ninth century tower at Bardsey, Yorkshire, where the
outline of the early porch is distinctly shown gablewise upon
which the later tower was built.

Invasions and Civil wars prevented progress during the ninth
and tenth centuries, but a revival took place in the eleventh,
when over twenty towers were erected in Lincolnshire and
many other notable churches and towers built elsewhere, including Bywell (21) and Ovingham in Northumberland, Burgh-
wallis and Kirk Hammerton in Yorkshire, North Leigh,
Oxfordshire, Deerhurst, Gloucestershire, and the fine towers
at Bosham and Sompting in Sussex. Of the same date

are the two extraordinary towers at Barton-on-Humber and Earls Barton, Northamptonshire (17). In the plan of the first the tower originally formed the body of the church with doors to north and south; to this was built a short chancel to the east and a narthex to the west, the tower thus becoming central. The chief interest of these towers rests in their decoration, this suggests a strong Norse influence and is a close imitation of timberwork in stone. These various examples of the early builders give to us a criterion whereby we may judge of the attainments in both architecture and craftsmanship in the days before the conquest.

With the invasion of 1066 the building of parish churches ceased for at least fifty years, for there was little time to give to the needs of the vills when castle and abbey construction took all available labour. During the latter half of the twelfth century this was gradually remedied and many small churches were built or repaired, together with a few of larger size, replacing those destroyed during the senseless excesses of the conqueror. The Saxon plan which was set out from one to three chambers, was continued, a tower sometimes placed over the central or quire portion. Indeed the plan became general during the twelfth century, as many central and axial towers were erected as western ones.[1] Central towers continued to be built during the entire mediaeval period, but for small churches they were the exception. Fine towers have been reconstructed upon twelfth century foundations as at Burford and Cassington, Oxfordshire, and at Gnosall, Staffordshire, but it is in the greater churches we find the usual central tower.[2] In the earlier centuries, owing to the required strength of masonry to support them, their erection often seriously interfered with the amenities of the interior, blocking the view into the chancel from the nave; it was not until the fifteenth century that the parochial interior was enhanced rather than spoilt by an axial or central tower.

The oolite stone beds found the principal material for a splendid series of spired towers found in the Nene valley and

[1] When we remember Arksey, Yorkshire, Barton, Westmorland, St. John, Devizes, Castor, Northamptonshire, Iffley, Oxfordshire, Sandwich, Kent, Old Shoreham, Sussex, Stewkley, Buckinghamshire and Great Tey, Essex, we realize how widespread was this type of tower.

[2] The thirteenth century Darlington; Leighton Buzzard, Bishop's Canning, Potterne and Witney; the fourteenth century Ashbourne, Caythorpe, Howden and Patrington and, in the fifteenth century, Cricklade and Gt. Bedwyn in Wiltshire, Thame and Minster Lovel in Oxfordshire, Ditcheat (36) and Crewkerne in Somerset and the fine towers in Yorkshire at Cottingham, Beverley St. Mary (34), Hedon and Hatfield to name but a few of the many.

the surrounding districts, these form the outstanding contribution of the thirteenth and fourteenth centuries to tower design. The roofs of early towers were intended completely to protect the walls in addition to throwing off the weather; this was first accomplished by a timbered pyramidical structure four-square on plan and protected by a covering of lead or shingles, as in the eleventh century tower at Bosham. As masoncraft developed, stone was substituted for timbering, partly as an insurance against fire, though at first, spire design still followed closely the earlier wooden forms fitted to the top of the tower enclosing the walls; this type was apparently confined to England and is the logical development of the protective idea, abolishing the treacherous guttering behind the parapets, which is a constant source of decay and trouble.

Although the broach spire followed the square of the tower it quickly changed to an octagon, the corners composed of half sloping pyramids from the square corner of the tower to the angle of the spire forming what is termed a broach; the broach was supported internally by corner arches called squinches which sometimes had a tendency to push out the walls. At first the spires were corbelled out from the face of the walls as at Ketton and Barnwell but later this feature disappeared. The broaches were often left plain as at Warmington, Pickworth (20) and Polebrook, Northamptonshire, or were masked by turrets or large pinnacles or both combined as at Bloxham, Wellingborough and Witney. A different method was to spring the spire from an octagonal top storey of the tower having the broaches below as at Barnack, Grafham, and the lovely example at Exton, Rutland, which is a perfect combination of setting out and proportion. At first the spire windows were confined to the lower part, but later were repeated in storeys and formed an ornamental feature. In the fourteenth century spires were further enriched by crocketed fillets following up the angles as at King's Sutton, Moulton, Lincolnshire, Oundle and Whittlesea. Another type of spire started within the parapet and was often connected with it by flying buttresses as at Coventry St. Michael, Louth, Rushden, Northamptonshire, Higham Ferrers (19) and Billingborough; the last with Weobley are excellent examples of reticent treatment; no promiscuous enrichment interferes with the natural aspiration to height and elegance. Timber-leaded and shingled spires were contemporary with stone but unfortunately have been largely destroyed, especially the ones which once adorned the towers of our cathedrals. There are good examples at Ryton, Durham, and at Sutton St. Mary, Lincolnshire, this last with lead spirelets to the corner

22 GRESFORD, DENBIGHSHIRE,
LATE FIFTEENTH CENTURY

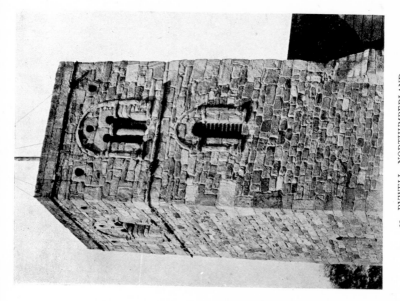

21 BYWELL, NORTHUMBERLAND,
TIME OF EDWARD THE CONFESSOR

A VILLAGE AMONGST THE YORKSHIRE MOORS

23   GRINTON, SWALEDALE, YORKSHIRE, FROM THE SOUTH-WEST

turrets; Westbury-on-Severn is an example of a tall shingled spire.

Towers of unusual plan and shape both round and octagonal are to be found; the first were built during the early periods, the latter more particularly in the fourteenth and fifteenth centuries. The early circular towers follow the Celtic tradition from Ireland where they were erected both for purposes of religion and defence. In England they were built for a like reason and seem to have been confined to the flint districts on the western side of the country.[1] The gradual disappearance of the need as a refuge did nothing to stay their continued erection before the thirteenth century. We must therefore look elsewhere for the reason of their popularity; this may be found first in the absence of good building stone and secondly that it was easier to build a circular wall composed of rubble or flints than to try to make a presentable angle to a square corner. There are roughly 120 round towers in Norfolk, 40 in Suffolk, eight in Essex and three in Cambridgeshire with an occasional one elsewhere. At Bramfield, Suffolk, the tower is detached from the church, having walls five feet in thickness; few are buttressed, and where found are usually of later date as against the oval towers at Beyton and Ramsholt. The ruined tower at Wortham is twenty-nine feet in diameter and still about sixty feet in height. There are numerous excellent twelfth century towers with good doorways and windows often set in a wall arcade, as at Saxham Parva and Thorington in Suffolk, and at Snailwell in Cambridgeshire. Saxham is a typical example nineteen feet in diameter and fifty-six feet in height; the Saxon Haddiscoe (18) is of the same height but within is but eight feet across. Many of the round towers were later enriched with belfries of octagonal form both appropriate and pleasing, as upon the fourteenth century Potter Heigham, and the fifteenth century Acle, Little Bradley and Rickinghall Parva; Ashby, although of the plainest, starts from the ground as a round tower but becomes octagonal for two-thirds its height.

Hexagonal and octagonal towers, unlike the round variety, are neither numerous nor are they confined to any one district; if we include lanterns placed upon the tops of square towers the number does not exceed fifty which are distributed over seventeen counties with a predilection for Northamptonshire and Somerset. A good round dozen are central as at Nantwich,

---

[1] East Lexham and Witton are tenth century; Bessingham, Colney Forncett, Gissing, Haddiscoe (18), Herringfleet, Howe and Norwich St. Julian belong to the eleventh century.

Cheshire[1]; of the others, few are octagonal from the ground up, they however show a diversity of form, from the pencil-like Fifield, Oxfordshire, to the beautiful Sancton and Coxwold in Yorkshire; this county was ingenious in its treatment of lanterns, shown at York on the towers of St. Helen and All Saints Pavement; this elegant example is planted upon a singularly plain square tower and is designed in the finest Yorkshire tradition, the elongated two-light windows fill in each wall between the delicate buttressing with their set-offs, pinnacles and grotesque gargoyles; the parapet is one of those lace-like designs for which the York masons were famous. These York lanterns are traditionally said to have been used to guide travellers through the forest of Galtres on their way to the city.

The majority of octagonal towers are of fourteenth century date, there is however a hexagonal example of the twelfth century at Ozleworth, Gloucestershire (25), while Uffingham, Berkshire, and Stanwick, Northamptonshire, are both of the thirteenth century. Many have the windows only on the cardinal sides, the alternate chamfers being hidden by pinnacles or turrets as at Lowick, Stafford, Upwell and Tong, Salop, this last completed by a pyramidal spire. The octagon was often used to bridge over the awkward join between a square tower and an octagonal spire as at Brayton and Patrington in Yorkshire. Lancashire has four of fourteenth century date at Aughton, Halsall, Ormskirk, and Standish rebuilt, all small square towers with chamfered tops to meet the octagon which forms the base for a spire; the first three have alternate lights, Standish however has a two-light window to every side. Nantwich, Sancton, Coxwold and Colyton have the same, excepting where a vice is taken up one side as at Nantwich and Somerton. At North Curry, buttresses occur at the angles, the squared base splayed to the lantern. There are several varieties; at Stoke St. Gregory the lantern is of two storeys, this also occurs at Wymondham. Windows to each face are usual in the fifteenth century, at Fotheringhay and Doulting, and the Yorkshire examples. When the octagon was employed as a western tower the results were less satisfactory; exceptions to this are at Sancton, Coxwold, Wickham Market, Stanwick and Hodnet, Salop; generally however this type of tower is too attenuated for the bulk of the church behind it, as at Fifield, Standlake and Cogges in Oxfordshire, also Bishop's Hull in Somerset. At Lostwithiel in Cornwall is a fourteenth century octagonal tower with a spire placed upon a thirteenth century base; it is French in design

[1] Colyton, Devonshire, Tong, Salop, North Curry and Stoke St. Gregory, in Somerset, St. Mary, Stafford and Bakewell, Derbyshire.

24 COMBEMARTIN DEVON, FROM THE SOUTH-WEST

25 OZLEWORTH, GLOUCESTERSHIRE

26 BRINKBURN, NORTHUMBERLAND, TRANSITIONAL DESIGN

with eight gabled double lighted windows, transomed by a band of carved tracery. Since its restoration by Street in 1883 it is decidedly more Frenchified than ever, and although beautiful, lacks the quiet reliability and charm associated with the best English work. In East Anglia at least fifty of the old round towers have had octagonal belfries added to them.

There were reasons why detached towers form an occasional feature of church planning; insecurity of foundations or instability of a central tower to withstand the swing of the bells. In this case separate bell-houses were erected, formerly at Salisbury and still existing at Chichester, Evesham and Bury St. Edmunds. There are several detached towers in East Anglia, the thirteenth example at West Walton is arranged as a lychgate in addition to a bell-house.[1] There is a group in Herefordshire which are primarily bell-houses;[2] several are partly constructed of timber as at Holmer and Pembridge, and at Newton and Skenfrith in Wales. Others entirely constructed of timber are at West Hanningfield, Margaretting, Stock and Blackmore in Essex, Upleadon, Gloucestershire, Marton, Cheshire, Newdigate, Surrey, Brookland, Kent, and Warndon, Worcestershire. Timber towers are perhaps more interesting internally than externally, for they are constructed of an apparently complicated timber framework of posts, tie-beams, struts and curved braces filling up the west end of the nave. At Mountnessing this is added to by trellis framing on the north and south sides. Many towers are built outside the church surrounded by an aisle with a lean-to roof from which springs the tower as at Blackmore, Margaretting, Navestock and Stock in Essex, on three sides at Marton, Cheshire, and arranged on plan as a Maltese cross at West Hanningfield, each addition with a gable roof. Others are constructed within the nave and carried up through the roof forming a spired belfry but kept free from the walls of the building, as at Laindon and Horndon-on-the-Hill. Two towers (if still existing) spring straight from the ground with pyramidal roofs, the first at Upleadon, Gloucestershire, with upright timbering, the second at Perivale Ealing, with horizontal boarding.

The use of brickwork for churches no doubt came through commerce with the Hanseatic League and made a fairly late appearance. It was employed where stone was scarce, especially in Essex and Suffolk. In the former county there is a fine series of fifteenth and sixteenth century towers which are in many

[1] East Dereham, Norfolk, Fleet and Sutton St. Mary, Lincolnshire, Tydd St. Giles, Cambridgeshire, and Beccles and Bramfield in Suffolk.
[2] Ledbury, Garway, Bosbury, Richard's Castle, Bronllys and Yarpole.

E

ways unique, lovely in colour, texture and form. The county was well known for its brickmaking from quite early times; the thin brick, as in most mediaeval productions, was beautiful because the craftsmen never knew "how not to." Rochford comes nearest to the ordinary tower with four-square buttresses and a fine octagonal turret overtopping the roof, however it is a little spoilt by having stone facings. At Sandon the tower is more sturdy, the parapets bastioned out upon a series of corbelled arches, the turret again topping the parapets. Both towers are decorated with vitreous brick, forming designs in black upon a red ground. Ingatestone (16) is a glorious tower of four storeys, four-square buttresses each with four off-sets. All mouldings and enrichments are in brick. The octagonal vice reaches the parapet, which is of Flemish character, rising by three steps at the corners to meet the turrets as well as in the centre of each face. At Fryerning the parapet is a combination of Ingatestone and Sandon, but the tower suffers from the diagonal buttressing which terminates half-way up. At Ingatestone (16) the massive buttresses give great dignity to an excellent design casting powerful shadows.

There are a few oddly designed towers. At Ormskirk, Lancashire, Great Urswick, and Cound in Salop they are large of girth and stumpy in height, designed as bell-houses, Ormskirk in 1540 to receive the bells from the priory of Burscough. Some towers have open arches to the west as at Cotton, Suffolk and Swinbrook, Oxfordshire; also astride a pathway as at Sandbach, Cheshire. In the curious central tower at Cartmel Priory, the belfry stage is set at right angles to the base so that the corners face the cardinal points. Although the construction is decidedly queer the effect is good, giving the building a marked character of its own.

28 BIRKIN, YORKSHIRE

27 RUDFORD, GLOUCESTERSHIRE

REMODELLING OF TWELFTH CENTURY FAÇADE

30 BREDON WORCESTERSHIRE FROM SOUTH-WEST

EARLY THIRTEENTH CENTURY IN THREE STOREYS

DARLINGTON EASTERN FAÇADE

SECTION III

ON FAÇADES

A BUILDING is distinguished or otherwise by the façade which it presents to the observing eye. Its elevation and characteristics should not only indicate its time and place, but the purpose for which it was designed and erected. A façade should not be used as a screen to mask the construction behind it, as happens in many Palladian buildings, where an entirely erroneous impression is conveyed as to what really lies behind an imposing frontage. This was also the case in a few mediaeval buildings but with this important difference, that it was never intended to hide the setting out of the church, but that the façade should serve as a wall screen upon which a magnificent sculptured iconostasis was placed as at Wells (12), where the doctrine of the church both militant and divine was shown for the benefit of all worshippers before entering the cathedral.

The façade or faces of a church should include its principal sides in addition to its gabled ends, for a church should be seen from all points of view; the chief interest should not of necessity lie at the west end, but might be provided for elsewhere, as at Selby and Lincoln. A series of individual methods of approach and treatment of this problem is exhibited during the progression of the centuries; the thirteenth and fourteenth were apt at designing the gable-end, whereas the fifteenth had no such splendours to offer, but excelled in the setting out of continuous aisles and clerestories, unified into a comprehensive and satisfying design. The same few elements were used in the setting out of gable and aisle, varying as regards position and size, according to the scientific development of the builder, and the century in which he lived. These elements comprised mouldings of base and parapet, buttress, window and doorway, the two latter arranged to fit the requirements within, and when possible kept in proportion to each other without. This aim was often difficult to attain, especially with doorways and windows in gable-ends, a problem which was greatly helped by the addition of side or aisle towers. In parish churches aisle towers are exceptional, a single western tower effectively obviating the need to design a western gable to the church.

The designs of the façades of the ninth, tenth and the first half of the eleventh centuries are largely conjectural, for Count William laid waste the land, and what building survived was later destroyed to make way for the ponderous and massive buildings which were part of his scheme of domination. In fen and borderland, dotted especially in the parts where revolt still smouldered, they became the outposts of his authority and power, and when necessary provided a refuge for his vassals in time of stress. His advent put back the clock for near upon a century, for it was that length of time before masons again built walls as close jointed and workmanlike as had been done in the early part of the eleventh century. This early Norman walling had little to commend it; even the ambitious size of the buildings erected and the gross weight of the materials employed were dull and unimaginative. The immense thickness of the walls was the direct result of the lack of building skill, shown in the use of small roughly squared stones (the weight an ordinary man could lift and carry) and the way they were bedded in a mass of mortar; the core however of both wall and pier was filled in with rubble mixed with inferior mortar. The number and size of the buildings undertaken were out of all proportion to the population of the country, and it became imperative to employ hordes of unskilled labourers working under the guidance of competent foremen, who no doubt came from Normandy, with the prelates and abbots who were destined to rule the many convents whose buildings were being so urgently pushed forward. In time, some of these unskilled men who had shown an aptitude for masoncraft became the nucleus of the permanent staff which each of the larger convents gathered round them, and the quality of the work improved.

Much of the traditional building methods employed in the dependencies of the Roman Empire lingered in the Norman work of the eleventh and early twelfth centuries; the strongly accentuated horizontal lines of cornice and string; the pilaster divisions of wall space, and the use of the groined vault and the round arch for windows, doorways, arcades, and stone roofs; all these features predominate in the earlier Norman building, but in a primitive form and with an imperfect understanding. Not the least glimmering is shown in this work of the transformation in construction which was to take place with the introduction of the pointed arch, a revolution which was to lift architecture from its pedestrian rut into something exciting and splendid, soaring upwards in daring and precarious achievements which, while the experiments in this new freedom were still fresh with a sense of novelty, had much the same effect upon the mediaeval mind as the skyscraper and the airplane have had upon the present generation.

The twelfth century façade was the direct outcome of the

unwieldy construction and the still unsettled state of the country, and the setting out was correlated with the main interior walls. These in monastic and cathedral planning were usually divided into three closely related storeys. The arcade or lowest storey was used as a means of communication with the aisles; the triforium or middle storey was the blank walling in front of the high-pitched aisle roof, and the clerestory or top storey was windowed to form the principal lighting of the church, for it was well out of the reach of marauders (67). For the purpose of lightening the weight of walling upon the arcade below, the triforium or blind storey was pierced by an arcade of its own, which in time became an important decorative feature of itself. For just as long as the aisle roofs remained steep in pitch, so long was a triforium necessary to hide the roof space, but, as the roof angle became less acute the need for the triforium disappeared. This triple horizontal division of the interior wall space was reflected upon the exterior façade, especially the gables of transept and quire, which if they remain as originally built will be found to have three tiers of windows, such as in the north transepts at Southwell and Winchester. This setting out was sometimes used for small churches where there was no interior dividing up of the wall space, such as the west front of the parish church of Iffley.

These tiers of windows are flanked and divided by rudimentary flat buttressing, which at the corners of a building may be termed clamp and elsewhere pilaster; they are broad, having very shallow projection, and usually without off-sets, dying above into the corbel table with which the walling is completed as at Birkin (28) and Kilpeck. The immense thickness of the walls, combined with the method of covering aisles with a groined or barrel-shaped stone roof, did not guide the stresses in any particular direction, therefore buttressing was not a structural necessity; indeed the pilaster buttresses of this time suggest decoration rather than use. A circular vice or staircase was sometimes constructed within a clamp or corner buttress, connecting the triforium, clerestory and roof with the ground floor; the extra projection given by the clamp then became essential. These corners of gabled façades were usually completed by heavy square turrets capped with pyramidical stone roofs; at first these were plain, but later received decoration as at Glastonbury, Tewkesbury, Bishops Cleeve and Bredon (30); they became octagonal towards the close of the period as at Ely from the ground up, or a combination of both as at Rochester. Windows were placed well up the wall to prevent ingress, for they were at first without glass, protected by wooden shutters;

in parish churches they were quite narrow with the deep wide splay within; if in the greater churches they assumed a considerable proportion, they were entirely without fenestration. As the semi-circular arch dominated all windows (44), doorways (55), arcades (78) and arches it circumscribed construction, keeping it in a builder's straight jacket, and effectually held back any attempt at scientific progress.

Few important western façades are left; the original form at Lincoln may be traced; it had three deeply splayed arches, the tallest in the centre with an elaborately moulded doorway at its base; the side arches formed part of the lower half of western towers. Tewkesbury is perhaps the finest remaining example; here again the design is a noble, deeply recessed arch of many orders, completely filling the façade and flanked by pepperbox turrets. How the original inner wall was completed is not known but would no doubt contain a finely moulded doorway with a window above. Western façades with attendant towers are at Southwell, Worksop and Castle Acre; the elaborated central doorway is a feature in them all. The twelfth century work apart from the towers has gone in the first two examples, at Castle Acre however more remains, the walls like those at Ely decorated with surface ornament, tiers of wall arcading of various heights and types; a monotonous and unimaginative form of enrichment showing a great lack of invention. The eastern ends of many great Norman churches were originally completed with an apse, as at Norwich (82) and Peterborough and formerly at Gloucester; these have all three tiers of windows, and from within are both noble and stately.

The earlier side façades are stark and grim, the decoration confined to pilaster strips and a corbel table (28); there is however little doubt that the rough walling was coated with a thin layer of plaster upon the exterior as well as inside, forming an adequate protection from the weather, and at the more important points colour was applied upon this base in red and yellow chevrons and zig-zag patterns round doorheads and other borders, which came later to be cut in stone.

The inordinate length of many of the Norman naves formed impressive side façades such as St. Albans, Ely, Norwich, Peterborough and Tewkesbury, notwithstanding that more roof was visible than wall. A little variation was obtained by using circular forms for the clerestory windows as at Southwell and elaborated corbel-tables at Kilpeck. The architecture of this first period cannot be considered inspired, it however excites interest in being the foundation from which sprang the later achievements.

NOT INTENDED FOR VAULTING

INTENDED FOR VAULTING

31 WHITBY, YORKSHIRE, NORTH TRANSEPT   32 RIEVAULX, YORKSHIRE, EAST END

TWO YORKSHIRE ABBEYS

33 RIPON CATHEDRAL, EAST END

The use of the pointed arch for the internal arcade had at first little effect upon the exterior façades; perhaps the pitch of the gable was a little sharpened, sometimes the window heads became a little pointed, but the three tier motive was not given up, and may be seen at Brinkburn (26) and Darlington (29) accompanied by clamp buttresses at the corners; the intermediate buttresses however are narrower and bolder in projection, chamfered at the edges and occasionally with off-sets. This is noticeable in parish church architecture, as at Ovingham, Northumberland, where we find the elongated lancet window to which northern masons were much addicted. Brinkburn Priory is an excellent example of the gradual change that was taking place (26); the eastern façade has three tiers of slightly pointed windows, the transept and nave long lancet windows with semi-circular heads, and the western façade three equal lancets, shafted and arcaded. In the south, New Shoreham showed a similar change of principle.

Gable façades were generally carefully designed in the thirteenth century, more especially in the interior; rib vaulting which would cover any given space with an even keel was now the controlling factor in the designing of the upper half of the exterior gable. At Whitby (31), where vaulting was not contemplated, it was comparatively easy to group the windows successfully, but where vaulting was employed as at Rievaulx (32), it regulated the height and form of the principal windows and made the exterior grouping more than difficult, as also exemplified in the transept façades at Salisbury (35) and the east end of Ely. If the interior of a gable showed two tiers of windows, the exterior showed three, for the top windows in the sloping gable lit up the roof space above the vault; it was therefore between these top windows and the principal lights where the hiatus occurred; this was caused by the space required for the internal vaulting, and made it well nigh impossible to produce a homogeneous design. The east end at Ely is spoilt by this endeavour to mask the break by blank windowing, unhappily continued on the buttress fronts; there is moreover a break in scale between the main windows and the upper storeys and the value of plain spacing is lost. At Salisbury (35) as at Ely the vaulting within breaks up the continuity without, but here the design is in four storeys corresponding to the setting out of arcade, triforium, clerestory and loft; there is no change in scale until we come to the sloping gable windows which are again spoilt by the continuous mouldings as they are at Ely.

The dividing up of the façades into tiers or storeys was a

throw-back to the earlier twelfth century form. At Beverley the double transepts, although split up into four divisions, do give a strong feeling of soaring; the lesser transepts immensely tall for their width, completed by attenuated gables, flanked by slender turrets whose stone capping overtops the finial between. Although the façades are broken up, the larger transepts are an improvement; these are completed by rose windows in the gables, a form of decoration used with superb effect in the west front at Byland, and in the transepts at York and Lincoln. The west front at Darlington succeeds only in the lower storeys with a fine doorway under a tall gable, the main windowing set in an arcade of narrow arches between the lights. The west front at Ripon has all the elements of a highly successful arcade, spoilt by the indiscriminate repetition of lancet forms on all three storeys of the flanking towers and by inadequate buttressing. The façade itself is well designed in three main storeys; at the base are three doorways under gables, the second storey has five lancets of equal height, the third five graduated lancets. This scheme fills the wall and is impressive within, but spoilt without by the towers with their grid-like decoration.

Thirteenth century design is altogether finer when it ignores the earlier breaking up of surface and grows in simplicity, relying upon proportions for effect. Before it reached this finality, however, many intermediate stages were tried out, as the two-tier north transept at Hexham, which again is finer within, the outside marred by the lowered gable. At Southwell east end are two rows of lancets, the lower stunted, but all of equal height. The exterior gable is as usual spoilt and the interior is not happy, for the level lancets fight with the curves of the vaulting. Lancets become arresting when they are of one storey and dominate the façade, as in the west fronts of Lanercost and Romsey, the north transept at Rievaulx, the east end at Boxgrove, and the magnificent "five sisters" in the north transept at York. These examples give an impression of inevitability, the perfect ensemble for which any other solution would be wrong. The lovely west front at Lanercost is a fine composition flanked by bold buttresses; it has a noble, deeply recessed doorway over which is a band of nichework giving scale to the design. The triple lancets which fill the main position are delicately treated, framed as they are in an arcade with narrow arches between, each window shafted and coupled, the centre light predominating. The gable of forty-seven degrees is shouldered to the side walls and contains a niched figure. The west front at Romsey has three tall graduated lancets under a containing arch, with a cinque-foiled window in the apex; the

34 BEVERLEY ST. MARY, YORKSHIRE SOUTH-WEST

35 SALISBURY CATHEDRAL, DOUBLE TRANSEPTS

36 DITCHEAT, SOMERSET, FROM THE SOUTH-WEST

37 EDINGTON, WILTSHIRE, FROM THE SOUTH-EAST

composition is severe and is without a doorway, it relies upon proportions for its effect. The east window at Boxgrove is of three lights beautifully spaced within to follow the lines of the vaulting. The finest thirteenth century façade of this type is perhaps the north transept at York, where the master mason was daring in his simplicity, filling this enormous space with five lancet windows. These are fifty-three feet in height and five feet in width; they have the advantage of retaining their contemporary glass. By their size and dignity they overpower their surroundings and impose their grandeur upon the observer by their simple austerity.

The display of the doctrine of the church was not of necessity confined to the interior of the building, but upon occasions was used on the exterior to impress and influence the more general public. Upon the western fronts of some of the great churches it took the form of a massive stone screen upon which the imagery connected with the teaching was grouped, placed in sunk niches under canopies. The finest example remaining is at Wells (12) where the west front forms a magnificent iconostasis of imagery tier upon tier. The lovely side towers and the massive projecting buttresses form a satisfying whole full of texture in light and shade. Seen in the early afternoon of a summer's day it is a noble composition, dignified and stately, remarkably simple in treatment without a trace of fussiness. The iconostasis was the peculiar English method of placing statuary upon a screen, in preference to the Continental grouping of the figures round the main porches.

The idea that this splendid screen was erected for no better purpose than to give a false impression of what lay behind is absurd, and is a worthy example of judging mediaeval work by the standards of the eighteenth and nineteenth centuries. The screen was erected for an entirely different purpose, and it was of small consequence if it interfered with the logical termination of the fabric, for its teaching was of greater importance than the aesthetic considerations which after all are a modern phase of criticism. Mediaeval work has all too often been judged by modern standards, standards which are often entirely alien to mediaeval thought and action. This external teaching was adapted at Salisbury and Peterborough and in the fourteenth century at Lichfield and Exeter. In the fifteenth century the iconostasis forming a great screen was taken inside and placed behind the main altar as at Winchester, St. Albans, St. Mary Overy, Milton Abbas and Christchurch Twyneham.

The west front at Salisbury is by no means so happy as at Wells; it is too much broken up, and the elements refuse to coalesce, neither the statuary nor the constructional parts predominating; the flanking turrets are moreover a poor substitute for the noble towers at Wells. If we compare the western façades at Lincoln, Wells and Salisbury, with Peterborough, the latter holds an exceptional place. The master mason of this remarkable façade was no doubt aware of Tewkesbury and possibly other examples now gone; with true insight he conceived the idea of three splendid arches under gables placed side by side and flanked by semi-towers, backed also by the towers of the western transept. These three gables are not as false as writers have tried to make out, for they are very much in keeping with the transept behind them, which was a western example of the nine altars eastern transepts at Durham and Fountains. This stupendous narthex or porch to the monastic church dominates its surroundings, as do the five sisters at York. It is a splendid portal to the massive, strong and almost endless nave to which it forms the introduction. The iconostasis here was grouped in the gables, where thirty figures mostly mediaeval stand in their niches looking down upon the scene, clustered about the rose windows proportioned to their setting.

At Peterborough the great western transept, of which there was once a second example at Ely, was matched at Durham and Fountains by great eastern transepts called in both cases the chapel of the nine altars, one now a ruin and the other seriously man-handled. At Fountains the centre gable has lost its original lancets, and at Durham the exterior walls have been shorn off to a depth of inches, the rose window re-modelled and the turrets invented. Both examples were an innovation which might have been developed, but they remain unique. The exterior of Durham nowadays is a little bleak and forlorn in spite of bold buttresses; at Fountains the two storeyed scheme is unified by its massive octagonal buttressing, giving a sense of height and strength; if the master mason had designed the whole in a single storey how magnificent would have been the result!

The side façades of the thirteenth century have more interest than that of the earlier period, the buttressing is bolder, the hidden flying arches were brought into the open connecting the aisle wall with the clerestory and bridging over the uninteresting roofs; windows took up more wall space and the mouldings of base and parapet were deeper, giving more light and shade. The side façades with triple windows at Ely and Salisbury (35) suggest, without, the form of the vaulting within, the triptych form of the window lights adding to their elegance. When vaulting did not enter into the scheme as in many parish churches, other forms were employed; the chancel at Ash-

bourne has two equal lancets between each buttress, that at Bre-
wood one, both equally successful; the chancel at Bamburgh
(Northumberland) is as elegant a design for a small chancel as is to
be found; here two lancets are placed between each buttress with
a fine corbel table above; four buttresses divide the east end,
and the priest's doorway to the south is within a steep and
graceful gable. More ordinary types abound, but rarely are they
either distinctive or beautiful; it takes something near to genius
to create a perfect building in its simplest form.

By the turn of the century the grouping of lancets and the
evolution of window tracery resulted in a less complicated
though richer treatment of the gabled façade; and it gained a
unity of design, that of a great window flanked by strong projecting buttresses. This simplicity was retrieved from severity
by the addition of crockets, finials and elaborated traceries. The
sturdy self reliant beauty under the gay flowering of the inven-
tive mason shown in such eastern façades as Lincoln, Ripon (33),
Selby, Bolton, Guisborough and Howden both east and west,
and in the north transept at Hereford, was less ascetic and more
human than in the preceding years. It all began rather quietly,
perhaps at Netley, where the eastern façade is plain and un-
assuming, with a two-light window with a circle in the head.
This plainness was a characteristic of early Cistercian building,
which nevertheless grew in delicacy and charm despite tenet
and creed. The façades at Tintern give a feeling of strength and
height, and for all their simplicity are both graceful and dignified, the south transept especially so, with its tall and slender
six-light window and the great gable above reproduced in
miniature over the doorway below. Without added decoration it is more arresting than all the piled up glories of the
eastern façade at Lincoln, where the windows are too large, too
wide as well as too short both for the façade and for each other.
The aisles there finish in gables which have no constructional
meaning, for behind them are but lean-to roofs. The horizontal
lines cut across the façade and tend to break its height, the
appearance of strength on the buttresses lost by overloaded
nichework.

A comparison between the eastern façades at Lincoln and
Tintern is instructive. The majesty of the eight-light window at
Tintern is magnified by its proportions, taking up as it does
over a third of the wall space. Above, the usual small window
in the gable fulfils its purpose without offering any rivalry to
the great window below. The buttressing has three gabled off-
sets without further ornament, and the ends of the aisles give
the design the expected lateral support. The north transept at

Hereford is a similar composition, height is obtained from the six-light window, flanked this time by massive octagonal buttresses.

It is however when we come to the work of the Yorkshire masons that we realize the true proportion buttress should have to façade, and the superb use of the crocketed and spired octagonal turret. In the unaisled quire of Bolton Priory there is a connecting link between the Yorkshire type and the south-western style; here the east window fills more than half the wall, a window once filled with a lovely network of tracery. The Yorkshire setting out is found in perfection in the quire façades of Ripon (33), Guisborough and Selby, the powerful buttressing being reminiscent of the early west front at Rochester, but refined and clarified. At Ripon the gable off-sets of the aisle and quire rise in progression, as do the octagonal turrets lifting the eye ever upwards to greater elevations. Except for the window tracery and the turrets, the façade is severely plain until we come to the top gable, where a disastrous Victorian restoration has gone far to mar the whole design. Guisborough has a similar eastern façade, a great window of seven lights flanked by buttresses with a deep projection of at least ten feet. The doubling of the main buttressing as well as that of the aisle is an additional feature of this design. Selby is in the direct line of descent, further enriched and elaborated. Shortly before the Black Death the Yorkshire masons had a spate of virtuosity, and the exuberance of their style is shown at Selby, Patrington, Heckington and in a less compass but with a still greater wealth of detail in the Percy tomb at Beverley and the chapter house at Southwell. The Selby façade is rich but is not plastered with meaningless ornament, for the enrichment is confined to the constructional features, flowing tracery and crocketed octagonal turrets producing a lovely composition. The next stage is at Howden where the east end of the church butted on to the market place; it is possibly the most elaborate of them all and the least satisfying. It formed an eastern iconostasis; in general effect however it lacks cohesion and is thin and fussy; the western façade of the same church is better with a fine use of enriched octagonal turrets. The east end of Carlisle follows the Yorkshire tradition without its sturdiness and strength, the tracery of the east window however is a magnificent composition.

In all these façades the great window is the predominating feature; internally it provides an immense area of glass for the painter craftsmen to exercise their art in producing their sparkling schemes of lambent colour; these windows formed the glorious background to many a high altar, taking the place of a constructional reredos. As yet the mason controlled the glazier, and though he left the long lights for him to fill as he pleased, he still required the glazier to submit to his dictates in the tracery, first of geometrical patterning and later with a sinuous treatment of tracery which must have been a joy to create, and to direct the flowing curves to form designs of leaf-like beauty.

Many eastern façades were broken by the addition of Lady and side chapels as at Tewkesbury, Exeter (96), Wells and Chichester. At Lichfield however the Lady chapel rose to the height of the main structure without actually becoming an integral part of it, as it did at Beverley and Worcester. It has an octagonal apse composed with three-light tall and slender windows placed between strong projecting buttressing, whose top slope is parallel with the slope of the windows; the effect is both rich and elegant and is as charming within as without, enhanced by the glowing foreign mediaeval glass with which the windows are filled. Unhappily this type of window was seldom used; it is however used on the west side of the north transept at Hereford, giving both height and grace where they are separated by stout octagonal buttresses, now completed by fanciful restoration tops. Towards the close of the period York produced an ornate western façade; it is a splendid example of ecclesiastical and civil pomp and as such adds greatly to the attractions of the city. But here are too many horizontal lines, and the towers' second range of windows is a mistake, levelling up to the great west window. The west window is a wonderful piece of designing embodying the Trinity and the bleeding Heart, the tracery retaining much mediaeval glass.

The west screen wall or iconostasis was continued during this time at Lichfield and Exeter; the former cathedral was greatly destroyed during the Civil Wars and has undergone more than one drastic restoration since those days. It is certainly a finer design than that at Salisbury, but in general effect is flat and monotonous, for it lacks light and shade. If the towers had overstepped the façade ever so slightly much would have been gained; as it is, the long wide surface of the wall with its tiers of saints clinging precariously to it is both tiring and tiresome. The front at Exeter is designed differently and assumes more of a screen to the portals than to the west front. It is but two storeys in height and does not interfere either with the west window or gable. It certainly brings the figures into closer contact with the spectator, but the dignified aloofness of the Wells series is gone.

The side façades may be divided into two distinct groups, those with aisles and those without, as at Lichfield, Hereford and Bolton, together with the fine series of three bay chancels. Bolton Priory is fortunate in having two styles, early and late. The south wall of the nave has six two-light tall windows with bar tracery; within is a passageway at the cill level. These windows are matched in the quire by five three-light tall shapely windows once filled with lovely free flowing tracery. The majority of side façades however had aisles and clerestories, the roof becoming less prominent and being sometimes bridged over by flying buttresses connecting clerestory with aisle. To support these, stout buttressing was required suggesting stone scaffolding, as at Exeter, where the nave has extraordinary projecting buttresses with set-backs and heavy four-square pinnacles to stay the flying buttresses which strengthen the resistance to the thrust of the vaulting (76). From an angle view they make a complicated setting, but viewed in elevation they support two fine series of traceried windows to aisle and clerestory. At Selby the stone vault over the quire was given up, but not before the square heavy buttresses had been erected on the aisle abutments, shafted with crocketed pyramidical tops. At Lichfield the buttresses to the nave clerestory stand behind those of the aisle, the flying buttresses less acute and not so good in effect. Against the quire at Ely the buttressing supports a two storeyed aisle (72), (75), including the triforium which is brought forward level with the aisle wall; above this they are continued with heavy pinnacles against which the flying buttresses are placed. Surrounded by all this stone scaffolding the true function of the side façade is somewhat lost in a mass of pinnacles; however the parish churches in the fourteenth century had unbroken chancels, usually of three bays, in which the dignity of the façade is regained, as at Heckington, Claypole and Patrington, in which tall and well designed windows are divided by excellent buttressing, and completed above and below by base mouldings and parapets. The windows may be two-light or three, geometrical or flowing.

The outlook of the fifteenth and sixteenth century masons changed from the ideal of building for its own sake to that of building for a given purpose. In the earlier periods the problem had been one of construction and strength; in this later time it was a question of producing a suitable setting for the crafts; especially that of the glaziers, whose coloured representations had won the popular eye, and who were clamorous for further opportunities for its display. Building construction was now sufficiently advanced to group thrusts at given points, thereby not only making the thinning down of the walls possible but providing large surfaces to be used as frames for the now fashionable glass.

Building during this last phase however was confined principally to the parish church, for no new abbeys or cathedrals were required; nevertheless numbers of them were either completed as at Ripon and Westminster, or remodelled as were the churches at Gloucester, Sherborne and Winchester, or entirely rebuilt as at Bath. Large chapels were erected in this latest style including St. George's, Windsor (124), Henry VII's, Westminster (126) and King's College at Cambridge (125); but the real contribution of this period was in the rebuilding of the parish churches such as the fine series along the east coast, extending from Yorkshire to Essex, also in the town and civic churches as St. Mary, Nottingham and St. Peter Mancroft, Norwich.

We have therefore to look for the output also in the alterations which took place during the last 150 years, both in monastic, cathedral and parish church—alterations which invariably had for their object the lightening and opening out of the building, by thinning down the arcades, abolishing the chancel arch, enlarging and multiplying the windows; for the interior of the church became, and rightly so, of more importance than the exterior of the fabric, thus reversing the dictum of the earlier periods of mediaeval architecture.

There are no longer lovely gabled ends to the buildings; gone is the simple solemn grandeur of Tintern east-end and the greater glories of the Yorkshire masons at Selby and Guisborough. Certainly the west ends at York and Beverley Minster are in the tradition with their twin towers, but from a point of composition their eastern façades are unattractive. At Beverley St. Mary (34) and Edington however the west fronts are admirably proportioned and good in detail without attempting a set piece. The difficulty of producing a satisfactory exterior proportion between doorway and window to match the interior needs had always caused trouble; at Edington the window is too short and it would have been better if the doorway had been combined with it. At Beverley St. Mary (34) the proportions of the window are splendid and the octagonal buttressing completed by open lanterns forms a delightful feature. The west ends at Holy Trinity, Hull, and Ecclesfield are windowed walls, the first with a horizontal coping, the second gabled; the west window at Westbury fills the gable well but the remainder of the façade is poor and skimpy. Again the west façade at Winchester shows a failure to grapple with the units forming the composition, for they remain uncoalesced and broken up, the horizontal grid across the lower part of the gable still further breaking up the design.

The side elevations however often redeem the lack of interest in the gable; they are generally a dual series of closely set windowing. The work of the master mason was to combine this somewhat monotonous repetition into a pleasing and dignified design, grouping the windows and taking full advantage of projecting buttresses, well moulded base courses and elegant parapets; these last becoming increasingly important as the roof line gradually disappeared from the eye of the spectator. The thrusting roof was not compatible with a high thin-walled and non-resisting clerestory, which was now usually steadied by a panelled beam roof, the construction of this particular type helping by horizontal beams, wall-posts and braces to clamp the opposite walls together.

Although this dual windowing is to be found in many districts in England, it was more successfully carried out in East Anglia, Yorkshire and the North Midlands.[1] The more successful setting out is to have two clerestory windows to a bay for one to the aisle below, and the less constructional interruption between each clerestory window the happier the result. By this means a more excellent proportion was attained than by repeating the single window of the aisle for the clerestory, as may be seen in the nave at Ripon, though an attempt has been made to differentiate between them, the aisle windows having three lights, while the clerestory is divided into five.

The clerestory differed from the aisle therefore in two particulars; in the number and arrangement of the windows and the setting out of the bay. Whereas the aisle bay was accentuated by the projecting buttresses and a deep moulded base course, the clerestory is usually without either; the one point in common was the parapet, essential to both. In districts where the clerestory was not developed, such as the south-west, the most was made of the aisle façade, as at Crowcombe, Somerset, Launceston, Cornwall, and Little Hempston in Devon, each county with its own peculiar setting out; but in all of them the run of windowing is divided by buttressing. To contrast Launceston with Little Hempston, is richness and severity; for the former is encrusted with surface ornament divided by pinnacled but-

<hr />

[1] Such examples as Blythburgh, St. Mary Bury, Lavenham (41), Long Melford (42) and Southwold (38) in Suffolk; St. Peter Mancroft, Terrington and Swaffham in Norfolk; Gedney, Billingborough, Boston and Sutton-on-Trent in Lincolnshire; Beverley St. Mary (34), Drax, Ripon, Rotherham and Tickhill in Yorkshire; to name but a few out of the many.

38 SOUTHWOLD, SUFFOLK, FROM THE SOUTH-WEST

39 GRESFORD, DENBIGHSHIRE, FROM THE SOUTH-EAST

FIFTEENTH CENTURY DESIGN OF THE SEVERN MASONS

40 NORTHLEACH, GLOUCESTERSHIRE, FROM THE SOUTH-EAST

tresses, while at Little Hempston the walls are plain with frowning battlements.

At Deeping St. James the earlier pointed arches over the heads of the windows are carried in front of them, to die against the buttressing; this early type was later followed up in Cheshire at Malpas and Bunbury north aisle, where a segment of an arc is employed to bridge the space between one buttress and another; in both instances the buttresses are of bold and deep projection. There is over elaboration at Bromham and Devizes; these south aisles are nevertheless charming in detail and their eastern ends form a striking and lovely design; perhaps one of the most satisfying is found at Mold, Flintshire, where the flattened four-centred exquisitely moulded head arches fill in the wall space in an admirable manner, the windows forming the walls between the buttresses; it is however always essential to success that sufficient prominence should be given to the buttressing, and that it should produce both light and shade.

In a clerestory of two windows to a bay there are several methods of treatment, Lavenham is continuous (41), as is Brereton and Barthomley in Cheshire. At Blythburgh, Gedney, Mancroft, Rotherham, Southwold (38) and Terrington there is a narrow buttress or pinnacle between each window; at Walsham-le-Willows, Newark and Swaffham the windows are inserted in the walling with a short space between each; at Audlem and Nantwich they are coupled by the bays. Where the windows match the aisle as at Denston and Malpas there is as much walling as window. A late and elegant clerestory design was evolved at Winchcombe (81) and Chipping Norton in the Cotswold district; this is square-headed in shape, each window of four lights framed by chamfered mouldings and bisected in twos forming a continuous windowing; it completely fills the wall space and is wonderfully light, leaving no ragged edges. Where an arched window did not fill in the wall spandrels of the bay, it was occasionally decorated with stone panelling. This had the advantage of allowing the window mouldings to be kept the full depth while the walling above was thinned down, the panelling becoming a decorative feature and sometimes following the lines of the mullions of the window below. This had been tried out with great success at Gloucester where the Norman walls of the quire had been hidden by a thin layer of superimposed stone panelling. It was also used in thinning the tower walls at Gloucester (5) and Malvern; it could be used in any position and was in reality blind tracery similar to the windows of the time, as exemplified in the clerestories at St. Mary Redcliff, Bristol (6).

G

During the last 150 years, mediaeval architecture did not remain static, but was continuously shedding the encumbrances and heaviness of the earlier stages of growth; it therefore became more and more "functional" and less "monumental" (to use modern tags) both in construction and design. However, unlike modern "functional architecture" it retained its interest and was seldom either boring or dull as is now so often the case. It was adapted and modified in various parts of the country, each adding its quota to the general sum, until it might well be considered to be the local in addition to the national vernacular; all this took place under the influence of the master builders, who were generally efficient and practical. National architecture only ceased with the advent of the individual architect, but even at the present day, the debt the modern architect owes to his practical foreman is a well kept secret, divulged to no man, and possibly unrealized by the architect himself.

This period must be judged not only by the adaptability of the builder to erect churches capable of housing unrivalled collections of glass and carved woodwork and showing them to advantage, but also by his internal contribution of the gorgeous stone fan vaults and the wonderful timber construction of the general mass of roofs. To these may be added the magnificent steeples dotted over the country which form so prominent a feature of the English landscape. This most adaptable of styles was constructed from a few simple elements, the art lying in the lay-out and the proportions of the whole. Unfortunately much of the work was piece-meal, and owing to circumstances but an addition to an already existing building, such as the fine clerestory at Nantwich placed upon the fourteenth century nave. This addition was however deplored by Sir Gilbert Scott, for it remains a curious fact that the Victorian architects, while approving and copying all the intermediate evolutions in the growth of mediaeval architecture, refused to accept its logical sequence and fought shy of its conclusions; perhaps for the reason that it was not sufficiently fussy and portentous to make it worth their while to emulate.

41 LAVENHAM CHURCH, SUFFOLK, FROM SOUTH-EAST

THE FIFTEENTH CENTURY IDEAL

42. LONG MELFORD, SUFFOLK, FROM THE SOUTH-EAST

EXTERNAL ARCHITECTURAL DETAIL

THE decorative form of what is but the detail applied to mediaeval construction has, by nineteenth century servile imitation,
brought the whole period into disrepute and contempt; for
present-day craftsmen cannot possibly produce work which was
first done according to ability and faith, in which the craftsmen
of one age, while guided by tradition, sought to improve upon
the work of their predecessors. This state of affairs enabled
them to produce a quality, which if at times rough, was
virile with an essential unity of purpose, in complete harmony
with the thought of their time and environment.

Technically the modern carver is far in advance of his fore-
bears; there is nothing he cannot accomplish with his hands if
he has anything to express; technique however is but a means
to an end, not the end itself; tradition vanished when the work
of the age was destroyed; therefore all that is now left to him is
either to copy self-consciously the work of earlier periods and
styles, or founder like a ship without a rudder; for the so-called
"gothic" revival, like that of folk dancing, was imposed from
without and had no roots in the common people, nor was it
circumambient, but foreign to the whole aspect of industrial
England. The only shop tradition a modern carpenter or carver
is taught is in keeping with his age, to smooth away the tool-
marks of his handicraft and to be mechanically minded, symmetrical and exact, suffocating to the intelligence and killing
all inspiration.

The colossal restorations undertaken during the Victorian era
(Sir Gilbert Scott restored over 700 churches, and there were
many more of his kidney) replaced the real thing with their
self-conscious imitation, for the method was ever "restoration,"
not preservation. In the examination of a church, therefore, the
first essential is to differentiate between the genuine, often
mutilated, original, and the smug replica; unfortunately in
many churches only the latter type remains, or if the former is
found, it has been carefully rechiselled or clawed to sharpen the
arrises and give to the mediaeval work a Victorian primness
and baldness. Again the church in the middle ages was sufficiently broad-minded to tolerate a certain freedom of subject,
which "a purified religion" could by no means swallow. At a
restoration at Chester two corbels in the quire were replaced

and four misericords destroyed to meet the ideas of the dean. In this volume we are not involved in a discussion of the merits or otherwise of the subject matter portrayed in mediaeval design; when however it enters within our province it will be noted. As the early explorers in so-called "gothic" discovered, details of carving illustrate and date work more easily than do masonry and construction, especially doorways, windows, mouldings and abutments.

WINDOWS

In the centuries before and after the Conquest the semi-circular arch governed both construction and design, from the great crossing arches and arcades at Chester St. John to a tiny piscina. At Hedingham, Essex, and St. Mary, Leicester, the sedilia and piscina are placed beneath round-headed arcades enriched with chevron ornament. The half-round was used over doorways, windows and wall arcades, also for surface decoration both within and without; the former in the chapter houses at Much Wenlock and Bristol, and the latter in the west transept at Ely. If the semi-circular arch be a sign of Norman construction, the chevron is certainly that of twelfth century decoration. Arches of every kind are loaded with it, especially doorheads, where often several rows are grouped in sequence; there is more invention than inspiration in all this surface carving, and at times the unmeaning enrichments pall with repetition.

In this round-headed age, each window opening stood alone, or if grouped they did not lose their individuality, e.g. as in the north transepts at Southwell and Winchester, where although designed in sequence they are separated by wide pilaster buttresses (28), (44), (67). Before the conquest, windows were small with an equal splay on both sides, and as far as we can judge, without enrichment. After the Conquest, however, owing to the coarse thick walling the splay came inside, the wooden shutters or glass filling kept close to the outer face, as at Ford, Sussex. The average parish church window was narrow and rather tall; there was more width however in the greater churches, as in the nave at Southwell, but a single window sufficed for a bay of the church, and these placed at considerable height to keep out undesirables.

At first windows were utilitarian, but were later enriched with shafts and carving, the head mouldings cut with the chevron as over the east windows at Beaudesert, Warwickshire, and Rudford, Gloucestershire (27); or with the billet round the transept clerestory windows at Ely and Winchester. The jambs were enriched by shafts with caps and bases placed near their front edge, the abacus of the capping carried on as a string at Winchester. The east clerestory windows of the north transept at Ely are grouped in a blind arcade of three, the window in the centre predominating and suggesting the oncoming of window design. The arcade motive is fairly common, found at Barfreston, Kent, and St. Peter's, Northampton. In the north transept at Kirkstall the two upper stories have each three round-headed windows connected by weather mouldings; this is carried a little further in the east window at Threckingham, Lincolnshire. At Fountains (45) the windows of the transept chapels are a further advance; two round-headed windows are connected by a string, above which is a circular window in close proximity.

The round-headed arch lingered over window and doorway after the pointed arch was used constructionally; at Kirkstall and Fountains, although the nave arcades have pointed arches, the windows and doorways remain semi-circular. So far there had been no serious attempt at grouping windows—the north transept at Warden, Northumberland, has a double lancet, but the south wall of the chancel at Ashbourne, Derbyshire, still shows a wall between the two lancets which form the setting out of each bay; they are however connected by weather mouldings. On the exterior of the north transept (66) three lancets are placed together with a continuous moulding, but within, the grouping shows triple shafted columns forming a lovely arcade in the best thirteenth century manner. There were many experiments in the unified window before any actual example occurs. The east end at Ely and the transepts at Salisbury (35) show equal lancets and also the tallest in the centre; here the masonry between each window has disappeared giving place to mullions forming a triple window, but as yet innocent of either tracery or a binding arch. The connection inside was more complete; in the Prebendal chapel at Thame, Oxfordshire, a charming interior arcade is placed in front of the triple window, completed above by semi-circular arched mouldings; at Pillerton Hersey, Warwickshire (47), the inner arch is pointed, with a quatrefoiled circular window within its orbit. At Ely, the exterior of the quire clerestory is in triplets covered by a moulded arch, while at Oundle, Northamptonshire, five graded lancets are combined under a pointed weather mould, the space between filled with ashlar slabs.

From this point the traceried window as we know it began at Ryton, County Durham; on the south side of the chancel is a curious round-headed window with two pointed lights, separated by a shaft with cap and base; the circular head and spandrel between the heads of the lights are cut from a single block, the spandrel with a sunk unpierced quatrefoil within it. At Cricklade, Wiltshire, is a complete window of three lights trefoiled with a plain circle above, the triangular spaces left solid. Other examples of what is termed plate-tracery include the chancel and south transept at Acton Burnell, Salop, a window at Ile Abbots, Somerset and at Norton, Gloucestershire; they are in two, three and four lights, but in all, the upper feathered circle predominates, the first three with three, the tracery heavily framed almost as solid as the walls; the masons soon grasped the advantages of two thicknesses of fenestration, the outer for the framing, the inner for tracery. There now followed a period in which every window was filled with geometrically designed tracery, where circles and triangles abound (48); these could be both appropriate and charming in such chapter houses as Salisbury, Thornton and York; but the average design, although architectural in motive, is often dull and hard. The probable reason may be found in the Victorian restorations, for this easy method of filling windows was exploited to the full; it was a thing after the restorers' own hearts, symmetrical and mechanical; it could be turned out with little effort, full sized details drawn out in the architect's office by the hundred, indeed, it was excellent practice for the premium-paying youngsters who largely formed the staff. It is however unfortunate that it is through this medium we are now asked to judge this type, which through renewal has lost its charm and become the stereotyped thing we see today. When used by a master mason and seen in its unrestored condition as at Tintern, we realize that its really disagreeable attributes have been largely imposed upon it in the nineteenth century.

By the commencement of the fourteenth century this rigidity of patterning was less pronounced, with more freedom of curve, while several fresh motives appeared; the reticulated or honeycomb used at Shifnal, Salop, West Kirby, Cheshire, and Sutton Benger, Wiltshire, the Kentish star at Beaumaris, Bedwyn, Chartham and Whitby. The use of the ogee curve did much to give interest to window tracery, the sinuous line taking a leaf or flame-like form, seen in the chancel at Nantwich, Cheshire, Great Harwood, Buckinghamshire, and Tickhill, Yorkshire. The windows were now broadened out, the head shortened into a four-centred arch. East windows were planned with from four to nine lights across, the tracery in the heads growing ever more intricate. The popularity of coloured glass had much to do with these enlargements, but the mason did not

3 DEERHURST, EARLY TENTH CENTURY

44 BIRKIN, YORKSHIRE, TWELFTH CENTURY

FOUNTAINS, LATE TWELFTH CENTURY

46 BRIDLINGTON, EARLY THIRTEENTH CENTURY

47 PILLERTON HERSEY, THIRTEENTH CENTURY

48 MIDDLETON CHENEY,
LATE THIRTEENTH CENTURY

49 LEDBURY FOURTEENTH CENTURY

50 FISHLAKE, LATE FOURTEENTH CENTU

release his grip on the tracery, compelling the glazier to fill these odd shaped openings by an exercise of his ingenuity.

A short list of greater windows gives the different qualities of this period; the east window at Ripon (90) of seven lights is geometrical with superimposed tracery, excellent to the point where the circle meets the heads of the lights, which leaves awkward spaces. In the free flowing traceried windows at Selby, Carlisle and York, the first two of nine, the last of eight lights, the ogee curves produce a sense of interwoven strength and growth, the patterning fused into harmony. The windows of this time show more imagination and resource in their filling than at any other period in mediaeval architecture. The tracery is usually lovely to look at, especially from the outside, and, when filled with plain glass admirable from within. When however coloured glass became the fashion the antagonism between the intricate tracery and the glass destroyed the merits of each.

This style developed local eccentricities, as seen in work in Oxfordshire at Dorchester, Ducklington and Cogges, where there is an unusual series of window tracery. The east window at Dorchester is divided by a stout buttress having three lights on either side filled in with reticulated tracery, each space for a single figure; across the lower tracery are carved a set of scenes from the Passion. Unfortunately the upper tracery has been completed by Butterfield to the Victorian formula. On the north side of the quire is a four-light window depicting the Stem of Jesse in stone; the central mullion rises from his body with stone branches crossing the intermediate mullions where are carved figures, supplementing those in the glass. The north aisle at Ducklington has four windows with from two to four lights having acutely pointed heads filled with complicated tracery, both difficult to cut or to fill; there is a similar square-headed window at Cogges.

A development of the thirteenth century arcade placed in front of the triple lancet windows took place later in the century, when a second or inner set of tracery was sometimes employed, as in the north window of the nine altars at Durham and the clerestory at Melrose. It was also used for the head of a window as at Broadwell, Oxfordshire, and Ditcheat, Somerset, where it forms a feathered arch. The head of the window was not confined to the pointed arch, the square-head was used with admirable effect at Skipwith, Yorkshire; a segment of a circle was employed at Byfield in the chancel windows, and the aisles at Over, Cambridgeshire, and Halston, Yorkshire. New features appeared locally, as the ball flower dotted on the framework of windows at Ledbury (49), Leominster and the south aisle at

Gloucester, but this fertility in design was suddenly crushed by the Black Death.

Before that calamity however there had been many signs of a new approach to window tracery design, the vertical line of the mullions being continued through the tracery to the head of the window. The east windows of Welwick of five lights and Fishlake (50) with seven, although designed in Yorkshire ogee and flame tracery, give a strong impression of upward growth, carried a step further in the aisle window at Hatfield in the same county, where the uprights run through the tracery to the head. At Edington, Wiltshire (37) the central mullions of the east window do the same, but at Nantwich, Cheshire, the change over is almost complete, for in the east window all vertical lines run through, without however producing rigidity.

The Severn Valley style, first adopted through necessity, had many advantages which craftsmen were quick to discover; it produced an admirable framework in panel form for the glaziers' canopied figures. An early example is the noble east window at Gloucester, and the glaziers' difficulties having been surmounted, there was to be no turning back, the panelled window continuing to the end, with only an occasional glance back to earlier forms. During the last hundred and fifty years window tracery was designed for the purpose of framing coloured glass, and by that standard it should be judged, as at Fairford, where the glass still fills (or did) the framework; to criticize it otherwise is to judge the frame without the picture. Aisle and clerestory windows should be considered as a range, not individually, when they often have a grandeur of their own as at Malpas, Cheshire, and at Lavenham (41) and Long Melford in Suffolk (42). In this period the number of lights was increased from three to four, the arched heads depressed, so that in many instances wall spandrels tend to disappear. For the east and other important windows the lights and tracery were arranged according to the subject matter to be chosen for the glass painter, who detailed the plan in place of the mason.

Transoms often divide the lights of a window by one or more bars; they are advantageous in strengthening the mullions and dividing the lights into panels. This feature is attractively used at Holt, Denbighshire, where the east window is crossed by a series of shallow semi-circles facing both ways, forming the base for the upper, and a head for the lower, lights. More ordinary examples are at Northleach, Gloucestershire, and St. Decumans, Somerset. In Cheshire the transom forms a base for the tracery, as at Malpas and Bunbury. Towards the close of the period the heads are flattened, as at Mold, Flintshire, or a seg-

51 CLIFTON REYNES, 1360

52 FRAMLINGHAM, FIFTEENTH CENTURY

53 LAVENHAM, CLERESTORY,
FIFTEENTH CENTURY

54 BUNBURY, CHESHIRE, 1528

55 ADEL, YORKSHIRE, TWELFTH CENTURY

56 HEDON, YORKSHIRE,
THIRTEENTH CENTURY

57 SHIFNAL, SALOP, FOURTEENTH CENTURY

58 HOLT, DENBIGHSHIRE,
LATE FIFTEENTH CENTURY

ment of an arch is employed as at Malpas; windows were also square-headed, especially for aisles and clerestories; such examples as those at Framlingham, Suffolk (52), Clifton Reynes, Buckinghamshire (51) or Porlock, Somerset, show how fascinating this type can be. There was more variety in design during this time than would have been thought possible, increased as it was by local characteristics. In the rough sandstone belt, cusping was almost abandoned, the tracery brought down, improving the proportions of the window (54). The last phase of window tracery is logical, fitting and architecturally good; it forms part of the whole, and was not an individual effort to decorate a hole in the wall, but by its vertical lines established its right to be considered a part of the architectural setting.

DOORWAYS AND PORCHES

Northumbria at Monkwearmouth provides our earliest example, for the western porch is contemporaneous with the building erected by Benedict Biscop in 674. Bede tells us that he brought masons with him from Gaul to build a stone church "after the manner of the Romans in which he ever took delight," and as far as we can judge the present porch formed a part of this work; it is twenty-one feet to the spring of the gable, but now forms the lower part of a later Saxon tower. It has four doorways to the cardinal points and within is covered by the earliest Saxon vault now above ground. All four arches are composed of a single row of through voussoirs carefully cut and fitted, and the sides are rebated for doors opening outwards, the east into the church, the north and south into destroyed cloisters, probably constructed of timber. The western arch is of a more elaborate nature with impost blocks, the jambs composed of upright slabs surmounted by others laid flat and bonding into the wall; the lower uprights are carved, and above them are twin turned baluster shafts placed on either side.

The chancel arches differed little from the doorways; the seventh century church at Escomb, County Durham, has a reconstructed arch made from Roman masonry in which upright and horizontal stones are used alternately. The tenth century Bradford-on-Avon, Wiltshire, is but forty-two inches across; the early eleventh century tower at Wootton Wawen, Warwickshire, has four small arches of which the northern formed an external doorway. At Corbridge, Northumberland, is a fine tower arch built of Roman materials dating from the second half of the seventh century. Representative doorways include the tenth century Earls Barton, Northamptonshire (17), the round

H

head of which is in two stones, the impost square and plain; framing the doorway is a pilaster strip, found also in the tenth century; Barton-upon-Humber and the eleventh century Stanton Lacy, Salop, and at Kirk Hammerton, Yorkshire. These arches sometimes show the first voussoir long and shaped to the curve as at Hammerton and Wootton Wawen; in later examples when there is above one ring, the first is recessed; when imposts project unduly they have been used for centring the arch.

Saxon constructional methods were continued for some time after the Conquest, especially in the smaller buildings, towers in Lincolnshire providing several examples. Romanesque forms had preceded the Conquest, for Edward the Confessor was busy remodelling Westminster anterior to the advent of Count William, who put an end to thin walling and tentative experiments. Owing to the thickness of the new walling a seemly doorway had to be devised; this was accomplished by recessing the arch in stages, as in the arcade, varying from one to seven, each ring having right-angled sides, decorated in the earliest stages by painting. The rings rested upon abaci dividing the jambs from the head though they followed its divisions, and were soon enriched by nook shafts with caps and bases (55). Shafts were multiplied with appropriate caps, first of the cushion type with surface ornament, later bell shaped. The right-angled rings of the arch had the chevron cut upon the face side, later upon both sides, meeting across the arris with a roll, and producing a richness of design.

The chancel arch and doorway had much in common in Romanesque and in pre-Conquest work; one was the entrance to the nave, the other to the chancel; it was principally a question of degree, but in the later style the chancel arch was the better proportioned and less liable to be overloaded with repetitive ornament. Hundreds of twelfth century doorways have survived, from the simple to the ornate. In earlier types a tympanum is a prominent feature, making a square-headed door and providing a suitable setting for symbolical carving. The majority of these designs are primitive and crude, although the prior's doorway at Ely, the south doorway at Barfreston and the west doorway at Rochester are pleasantly decorative.

Doorways are frequently framed in a gable, as the interesting south doorway at St. Margaret-at-Cliffe, or provided with a square frame, as in the unusual example formerly the entrance to the chapter house at Kenilworth. The gable was projected into a semi-porch to enable more and more rings to be added. At Adel, Yorkshire there are five (55); the west doorway at

60　SOUTHWELL, NOTTINGHAMSHIRE

59　WELLS, SOMERSET

St. Germans, Cornwall, has seven. Porches are uncommon; however, good examples are at Selby, Southwell, and a splendid one at Malmesbury. Parochial porches occur at Bredon, Worcestershire, and Tortington, Sussex, but with the exception of Malmesbury none call for particular remark. In the last decades of Romanesque varied forms of enrichment came into use; the medallion with the signs of the zodiac or scenes figure in the north doorway of St. Mary's chapel at Glastonbury, showing a remarkable advance in power and execution; other instances occur at Fishlake, Yorkshire and Barfreston, Kent. At Kilpeck, Herefordshire, the jambs are decorated with convolutions in which knights battle with dragons. Now and then a doorway is designed without an architectural break between arch and jamb, as the west doorway at Iffley, Oxfordshire, where three concentric rings of ornament are taken round the doorway, two of them with beak-heads. At Stillingfleet, Yorkshire two rows of chevron meet at the arris with balls in the spacing; however this redundance in twelfth century work faded out with the advent of the constructional use of the pointed arch, and mouldings were developed giving a strong contrast in light and shade, adding to the dignity of doorways and porches.

The round arch continued in use for some time; it is found at Weston, Hampshire, Edleston, Staffordshire and Spratton, Northamptonshire, where late ornament is still employed. In the transepts of Hedon south and Ripon north the round arch continues but with new mouldings. When the shape did alter it soon became acutely pointed as at Ashbourne, Derbyshire, Hedon (56) and Wells. Beverley Minster has interesting half-way examples to both transepts with semi-circular doorways flanked by acutely pointed arches; the foundation of the mouldings retained its right-angled shape for a time but this quickly disappeared. The setting out of the doorway arch with two pointed openings with a spandrel above is common to the greater churches as at Chichester, Salisbury and Westminster Abbey. In parochial instances the heads sometimes have trefoils as at Shifnal, Salop (57) and Hedon.

There are several excellent porches of thirteenth century date both single and two storeyed; there is one of each at Uffington, Berkshire. Other two-storeyed porches are at Wells and Salisbury; the former is the earlier and better proportioned with an interesting inner wall arcade. Salisbury is unfortunately the prototype of "Victorian Gothic" so beloved of Street, who copied it with exacting care in the Law Courts in London and was also responsible for turning many a pleasant village church into a petrified version of this type, thereby proscribing the whole style. Before the west front of Ely is a sumptuous newly carved porch combining within the glories of this time; it has double arcading to the walls, both doorways divided by a central pillar holding feathered arches, with an open traceried spandrel above. When the porch was examined by Essex in 1757 it was so dilapidated that he advised its removal as an incumbrance not worth the keeping. The nineteenth century however so thoroughly restored it that it is now useless as a guide to the work of the period. At Bridlington Priory within the north porch is beautiful unrestored detail in the trefoiled wall arcades and caps, the inner doorway with delicate carvings. Dog-tooth ornament, the descendant of twelfth century nail-head, was the one surviving enriched moulding, as at Hedon (56); later however at Bridlington it turned into a rose cunningly devised; the gable head enclosing the doorway was continued, acutely pointed at Darlington, less so at Ripon.

With the close of the thirteenth century the style broadened out with fresh motives, as in the splendid doorways to the chapter-houses at Hereford, Southwell (60), Wells (59) and York, work which for elegance and grace in handling are difficult to match; the south-east porch at Lincoln may be so classed in spite of drastic restoration, for of its kind it is unique in England. On the north side of St. Mary Redcliff is a three-storeyed hexagonal porch which in its early days must have been magnificent both in plan and detail. Harvey states:—

"the sculpture like most of that which adorns the exterior of the church is a modern reproduction of ancient work perished beyond the possibility of preservation."

The average porch of this time had few outstanding features, but is usually substantial and plain; Byfield, Northamptonshire is flanked by shafted pinnacles, with an ogee arched weather-mould. The south porch at Patrington, Yorkshire is of two storeys and entirely depends for its effect upon proportion and balance, in which it does not fail.

After the Black Death however porches grew in importance; they were erected in connection with the greater churches at Hereford, Gloucester, Canterbury and Beverley Minster (p. 12), but the majority are closely related to the parish church. They are built in one to three storeys and formed the main entrance for ordinary occasions; they were used for legal transactions and other business and filled in an essential part of the communal life. The horizontal or slightly cambered parapet now replaced the gable, the porch becoming four-square, and although the general outline was fairly constant, the detail is treated in a variety of ways; buttresses are four-square, octagonal or diagonal, with or without pinnacles; the doorheads usually surrounded by a square frame with carved spandrels. It is more than difficult to select particular examples for criticism or praise. The Cotswold type at Northleach and Burford is well known. The flint porches of East Anglia decorated with flushwork are surprising in their effective handling of flat decoration (63). Those of Devon and Somerset are square, plain and strong; the brick examples in Essex (64) and those in timber, together with the pleasing porches in Cheshire, show an almost unlimited capacity for design of the first order. The more interesting porches are those of two storeys where there is a façade of sufficient height to group the details into a unified design. Niches are almost indispensable; at Southwold, Suffolk, they are placed between the windows; at Northleach in the centre, in two tiers; at Woolpit, Suffolk (61), in a charming group of five.

At Bramford, Suffolk, the decoration is confined to the doorway, parapet and buttresses and except for a niche the rest is severe; at Launceston, Cornwall (62), every inch of the surface is carved both front and sides, yet both examples are beautiful. At Doulting and Mells, Somerset, the parapet takes an acute ogee curve to a central niche. At Beverley Minster the north porch is panelled throughout (now unfortunately filled with Puppetry) the parapet with horizontal nichework. Gloucester also accentuates the horizontal line by a series of canopied niches across the upper storey. At Hereford the north porch is distinguished by octagonal lanterns at the corners, with an arch to each side of the porch. Porches form an attactive feature of fifteenth and sixteenth century building; in this they outshone the doorways, although successful schemes were employed to enhance the usual small English entrance. To do this, side canopied niches were essential, either placed below the window string, or with the spires climbing up and connecting the window with the decoration below as at Kingston St. Mary, Somerset. Semi-porches were occasionally designed as at Maids Moreton, Buckinghamshire, where cones of fan vaulting spring up from the jambs. Later doorways and porches usually have flattened heads with carved spandrels, enriched with label-stops and cusping. Cirencester (65) has an exceptional entrance into the church in the three-storeyed south porch which once formed the Guildhall of the town; it is three bays in width, the windows bayed, the walls panelled, the parapet pierced, and the buttresses niched; the whole forming a charming link of the finest character between religious and domestic architecture of the period, for it is an imposing and handsome entrance façade to an elegant and comely church.

MOULDINGS AND ABUTMENTS

The mouldings employed during the mediaeval period for base, parapet and the framework of window and doorway show a gradual advance towards maturity as well as an increase in dexterity; just as the shape and strength of the buttress gives evidence of a scientific grasp of thrusts and abutments. These in the Norman period were primitive, for the groined roof required little additional support. The pilaster buttresses were probably a decorative feature designed to relieve the monotony of bare rugged walls; they were wide and shallow without offsets, dying into the parapet above and into the base below, framing large square panels of walling, one to each bay including a window to match (70). At times the edges were enriched with a bull-nosed moulding and later the whole buttress was occasionally designed in half-rounds as those placed against the chancel at Berkswell, Warwickshire (67). The parapet, like the buttress, was plain with the exception of its lower edge which was set out either with corbels, arches or both combined. In small churches such as Elkstone, Gloucestershire, and Kilpeck, Herefordshire, the corbel table is without arches, but is nevertheless enriched with a billet or a chevron. In the greater churches small arches bridged from corbel to corbel with additional enrichments as at Ely, Southwell and Winchester, or with double arcades as at Romsey. Corbels were usually carved with grotesques, fabulous beasts and horrid monsters exhibiting grim and cruel satisfaction, evidently a characteristic of the age. Crocodile heads terminate many label stops, especially in Gloucestershire and Worcestershire. Arcading is also the only method of covering the walls, used as decoration either singly, or in tiers, placed upon towers, gables and aisles both within and without.

With the constructional use of the pointed arch the buttress became an essential element in combating the constant thrust; more and more did it shoulder and steady the structure by relieving the pressure of arch and vault until, by the fifteenth century, it would have been feasible to build a skeleton church without exterior walls, for thrusts were safely conveyed to given points and secured by buttressing. Underlying the development of mediaeval building was the constant endeavour to minimize the thrust of arch and vault and to render the building stable. This was helped by carrying the weight of the

FIFTEENTH CENTURY PORCH DESIGN IN FLINT AND BRICK

64 RAYLEIGH, ESSEX

63 KERSEY, SUFFOLK

65 CIRENCESTER PORCH

main vault from the clerestory to the aisle buttresses by means of flying stone arches, the aisle buttresses heightened, strengthened and weighted down by heavy copings or pinnacles to keep them steady. This method can be studied at Salisbury and the quire of Southwell.

At the close of the twelfth and the first half of the thirteenth centuries the shape of the buttress varied; clamp, square, chamfered, octagonal or a mixture of them all. Clamp is found at Lanercost and Darlington (29), a chamfered square at Southwell, an arcaded square at the east end of Ely and octagonal in its western porch. The majority of parish churches have however plain buttressing with one or two off-sets, sometimes of gable form, the base mould a simple slope to throw off the weather, the parapets generally plain. In the greater churches mouldings are elaborated, with several slopes to the base and additional strings above; at Salisbury there is another set at cill level (71). When pinnacles are employed in place of copings they are often thin attenuated illbegotten things; at Salisbury they are particularly obnoxious—made of wiry-looking shafts, with top heavy cappings; the same ugly combination is at Ely, and the squared turrets at Darlington are little better (29). It is perhaps unfair to hold thirteenth century masons responsible for these unsightly things, for to all appearances they belong to Victorian ingenuity.

With the close of the thirteenth and the early fourteenth centuries architecture was throwing off its growing pains, and for a short time the masons devoted themselves to making the best of both worlds, giving all they knew to the church, adding to its beauty, and, at the same time doing it for the glory of man as well as God. It was a holiday between the earlier training and the later responsibilities, and the masons and artificers revelled in it, creating loveliness because for a short space it was both in the air and in the blood. No buildings can vie with those erected during these fifty years. We have only to note the quires of Bolton, Guisborough, Ripon, Selby and Tintern, the chapter houses at Southwell (114) and Wells together with the cathedrals of Exeter (76) (96) and Lichfield, to realize how rapidly the sensuousness and beauty of building had taken the place of monastic aloofness, for the earlier severity and austerity was softened and warmed into graciousness. After the Black Death architecture became more functional and scientific in its aims, but for this short spell the search for beauty prevailed, both masons and craftsmen guided and endowed by the benevolence of the princes of the church.

In the fourteenth century the parochial buttress and base

mould were similar to that of the preceding period, the mouldings less deeply cut and the off-sets often gabled. In the greater churches the corners became an important architectural feature, the buttresses facing each way (68), completed by gables and crowned with large open turrets having cusped spires as at Howden and Selby, two to the principal gables and two lesser ones for the aisles. During this period flying buttresses were employed as at Exeter (74), Ely (75), Malmesbury and Westminster, the last an almost complete example of the French stone scaffold. At Exeter (76) the aisle buttresses are projected deeply, steadied with heavy copings surmounted by weighty pinnacles. At Ely (72) owing to the triforium having the same face externally the buttresses have an added height, steadied by enormous square pinnacles. At Malmesbury the tops appear behind the parapet. Parapets varied, either moulded and solid, or openwork, with a flowing feathered ogee at Malmesbury and Selby, triangular at Heckington, Tewkesbury and Redcliff (6), or trefoiled at Lichfield (68). Window frames are many membered, the weather mould often of ogee form cusped, and sometimes rising above the parapet as at Nantwich. Canopies with ogee heads, strings and arcades decorate the exterior.

With the Black Death all this rich splendour ceased, and until the Suppression building was concerned with needs and requirements, building in the true sense of the word, well-proportioned and fulfilling the essentials for which it was designed, a framework for the skill and cunning of the craftsmen.

During the fifteenth and sixteenth centuries buttresses were employed not so much to abut the vaulting, which was now less thrustful than before, but in support of the outer walls now largely composed of windowing; the inner walls with slender arcades upholding clerestories with large windows. Timber roofs seldom exerted thrust, for in this latest clerestory design they were of the beam type; their function was now to hold together the anatomy of the building, and provide additional light and shade to the otherwise flat surface. This may be studied at Bromham, Wiltshire, Lowestoft, Suffolk and Gresford (69), Denbighshire, the buttress projecting well forward averaging eighteen inches in width. In many examples it springs from base mouldings in which hollows and ogees are combined; continuing with off-sets with well-designed slopes, sometimes slightly cavetto in form. The heads are treated either as a narrow pointed gable with a slope behind reaching to the parapet, or as an ordinary off-set from which springs a pinnacle set edgeways reaching above the parapet. The front of the

SHBOURNE, QUIRE, THIRTEENTH CENTURY   67 BERKSWELL, CHANCEL, TWELFTH CENTURY

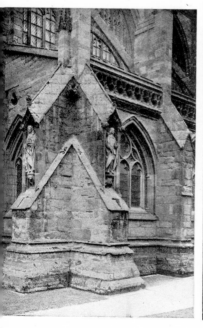

LICHFIELD, FOURTEENTH CENTURY   69 GRESFORD, FIFTEENTH CENTURY

70 ROMSEY, NORTH TRANSEPT,
TWELFTH CENTURY

71 SALISBURY, LADY CHAPEL,
THIRTEENTH CENTURY

72 ELY, QUIRE, NORTH
FOURTEENTH CENTURY

73 BRANT BROUGHTON,
FIFTEENTH CENTURY

buttress is often panelled or has a canopied niche or flushwork and forms a distinctive addition to the façade.

Base moulds vary, Little Hempston, Devon, retains the earlier single slope; Launceston (62) is enriched with a band of carved quatrefoils, as is St. Lawrence, Evesham, with a second band above. There is occasional flushwork in East Anglia as at Worlingworth, and carved panels with shields at Hoxne, Suffolk. Terrington St. Clement and Rippingale have deeply moulded bases with quatrefoiling; Gresford (69) and Mold are enriched with a second set at cill level. The base became a visible footing by which the walls were steadied and strengthened forming an important part of the decorative scheme.

The parapet however received the greater attention; the battlement is a common form, with mouldings across the horizontals or taken completely round the merlons, and sometimes enriched with tracery cut in the solid; examples are at Baynton chapel, Bromham, and Lavenham (41) with shields; openwork types are at Fontmell Magna, Dorset with diagonals; Stoke St. Gregory and Batcombe in Somerset with quatrefoils set in squares; Redcliff (6) with trefoils and at Blythburgh with quatrefoiled circles. The pinnacles which crowd some parapets are suspect; mediaeval examples have perished; they were always liable to destruction by tempest and man; even when originally erected they must have been something of an anachronism, a childish conceit, like the baberies under the stall seats. They require constant attention, for iron dowels used to secure them rusted and burst the stonework asunder. The pinnacles we now see are modern, often ill-designed and poorly cut. Parapets are distinguished from the walling by a string, usually a hollow moulding from which at intervals gargoyles are projected, used for shooting the surface water from the lead flats. The hollow is now and then dotted with patera, flowers, leaves, or little animals and birds, seen in profusion at Gresford (22), Mold and Tarvin. Magnificent octagonal turrets with stone cupolas flank the gables of many great churches and chapels of this date, at the east end of Winchester (77), also at St. George's, Windsor, and King's College, Cambridge, and with open lanterns now remodelled at Beverley St. Mary (34).

I

THE INNER TREATMENT OF THE MAIN WALLS

The main arcades of the average parish church, although the direct result of necessity, formed an important decorative feature. One of the charms of mediaeval architecture lies in the manner in which utilitarian objects were transmuted into beauty without losing the essential purpose for which they were created. A church without arcades is lacking in one of the intrinsic characteristics of a mediaeval building, without light and shade, and the complicated and elusive vistas which are so pleasing to the ordinary intelligent being, who without the technical knowledge of architecture or an understanding of its nature, may still appreciate the results just as in the same way music may appeal to the mind without a knowledge of counterpoint or composition.

The arcade or a colonnade of piers and arches is in direct descent from the Roman and Byzantine periods; it had formed an essential part of their basilicas, which later were adapted for Christian worship; they were indeed the nucleus from which the church gradually evolved its own structural requirements. The difficulties experienced in roofing over wide spaces, and the additional need in northern climes of having a roof sufficiently steep to throw off the weather, were important structural reasons for the perpetuation of arcades in planning a church. Aisles, in addition to serving as gangways, had also a liturgical significance for processions and later in the multiplication of altars and chapels.

From quite early times only the greater churches had aisles, as shown in the remains of the seventh century church at Brixworth, Northamptonshire; this church, although of basilican form had no rows of pillars, for the aisles were connected to the nave by arches cut through the solid walls, a method employed occasionally in later times. The eleventh century church at Great Paxton, Huntingdonshire, however, has excellent arcades, an example of how far our architecture had advanced before the Norman throwback. Arcades were after all used primarily as a means of communication between different parts of the same building in an endeavour to make the church homogeneous and overcome the constructional difficulties, but this was not quite successful before the fifteenth century.

Arcades erected in the twelfth century are usually part of the original build, and not, as many later arcades appear to be,

74 EXETER, NAVE, FOURTEENTH CENTURY

75 ELY, QUIRE, FOURTEENTH CENTURY

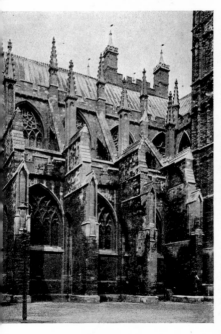

76 EXETER, NAVE, SOUTH,
FOURTEENTH CENTURY

77 WINCHESTER, QUIRE,
FIFTEENTH CENTURY

78 ST. BARTHOLOMEW'S SMITHFIELD, LONDON

an afterthought when the church was enlarged piecemeal. Such examples as St. Nicholas, Gloucester, Longford, Derbyshire, St. Chad, Stafford, with short sturdy piers, and Kirby Lonsdale (89), with tall piers, influenced from Durham, were so erected at the beginning, and draw attention to the heaviness and apparent solidity of twelfth century lack of technique. All these piers are connected by semi-circular arches with or without chamfered or other mouldings; large numbers of twelfth century arcades have survived in abbeys and cathedrals owing to the herculean task involved in their removal when more enlightened and cultivated masoncraft was available. In the transepts at Winchester, stripped of their original plaster, may now be seen the early wide jointed masonry, and later arcades with round, square, or moulded arches and piers are still in bulk at Hereford, Durham, Southwell and Norwich (82), to name a few; Gloucester, Tewkesbury and originally Pershore have cycloptic piers of great girth and height.

Twelfth century arcades are seen to the greatest advantage in such abbey churches as Buildwas, Ely, Peterborough, Romsey and Waltham, where monotonous repetition has a grandeur of its own, if it does become heavy and inert, lacking in both imagination and inspiration; when first erected however it was coated over by a thin layer of plaster upon which were painted repetitive patterns of chevrons, billets, reeds, diamonds and whorls, coloured in red and orange, brightening up both piers and arches with an odd fantastic effect. The lighting of these cavernous Norman churches was none of the best, and although the painting may have been gaudy, the effect must have been subdued, especially if the windows contained any coeval glass, which although rich in deep colours was opaque and thick in quality.

The parish church derived its arcades from the churches of the monks and canons; we have already noted that Kirkby Lonsdale (89) copied Durham, just as Frodsham was in direct line with the collegiate church of St. John in Chester. Both examples are above the average height, for the arcades were low, the spacing governed by the strictly limited scope of the semi-circular arch employed. There was little attempt at a proportionate scale either in relation to the church or even of itself; fortunately individuality was attained by the haphazard method of its planning, always an antidote to the deadly dullness which mechanical exactness produces either in building or craftsmanship.

The majority of twelfth century piers are cylindrical in form, alternating with those of octagonal or square design; if the latter they are relieved by moulded shafts placed at the corners, as at Whaplode, Lincolnshire. At Ely and elsewhere there are two arches to a bay, the pier between of circular shape, the main divisions square with moulded shafts. The bases at Frodsham, St. John, Chester, and St. Cross, Winchester are square and of considerable height, connected to the circular pier by a ring of shallow mouldings. The early caps matched the bases, square in shape and enriched with cones and reeds. Later they became circular and of cavetto shape with incipient foliage sprouting from the cones, or with Celtic strapwork as at Hereford. Arches do not often exceed two orders (89), (79), the edges kept either square and sharp, or with a fillet or roll mouldings; they are also chamfered, and in the later examples are decorated with borders of chevrons and billet mouldings carved in the stone; these may be seen at St. Chad, Stafford, and Walsoken, Norfolk; or they may have scrollwork painted upon the chamfers as at Kelmscot, Oxfordshire. Twelfth century arcades owing to the thickness of the walling, the girth of the piers and the lowness of the arches, afforded little more than a passageway between the nave and aisles, and I suppose this was what was aimed at. Certainly the small size of the aisle windows did nothing towards lighting the nave, which had to rely upon other sources for its supply.

By the middle of the twelfth century the pointed arch made its appearance at Great Bedwyn, Clun, Ramsey, Old Sodbury and Waddesden, lightening the arcades, although the round arch still remained in use as at Frodsham, Kelmscot, Walsoken (84) and Whaplode. The difficulty of the first half of the twelfth century however lay in the poor quality of craftsmanship, where bulk was mistaken for strength, and the stone cutters and masons' amateurs, instructed by a few experienced foremen; this is surely an early example of mass production as we know it today, where inexperienced employees are gathered irrespective of capacity or talent. Nevertheless the twelfth century is not without interest, showing the rudiments culled from the fragmentary ingredients of earlier styles, and foreign ways of working being forged into a malleable form which had in it the germ of the later developments.

The employment of the pointed arch for constructional purposes was the beginning of mediaeval architecture; it had already appeared as decoration, but not until it was used as a means of solving the problem of vaulting over an uneven space, keeping an even keel, did it show the possibilities inherent in its adoption. Freed from the round arch, there seemed little reason why the builders should stay their hands at the old heights; for the pointed arch was malleable, not rigid, it could be heightened or widened at will, and for a time the masons enjoyed this new freedom, especially in such buildings as Salisbury and Worcester. No such magnificence could, however, be attempted in connection with the parish church; the change was shown in steeply graded arches as at Corbridge and Holt which harmonized with the tall narrow windowing of the time.

The constructional use of the pointed arch accelerated the evolution from Romanesque to mediaeval architecture; although in certain districts the time-lag was considerable and was nowhere uniform either in time or manner. Sometimes the piers remained untouched whilst the arches became pointed; in others the piers were thinned down and grew in height while the arches continued semi-circular in shape. At Hatfield, West Riding, Yorkshire the tall circular piers have cavetto-shaped caps completed above by large square abaci, the whole arcade with pointed arches and chamfered members. The quire at Hedon and the nave at Hartlepool have decorative qualities culled from the churches at Hexham and Selby; the Hartlepool piers are square on plan with keeled or half circular shafts on the cardinal faces; the hollow cappings worked to the shafts below and spreading to a broad circular abacus above; the arches deeply moulded but not disagreeably ribbed. Darlington shows the completed change, where are a variety of pier designs in the same arcade, circular, octagonal and shafted with capitals to match, the arches having three chamfered members encircled by a weather-moulding.

Arcades were no longer only a means of communication, but an orderly development of masoncraft, growing lighter, taller and more elegant with less obstruction to the view. In the thirteenth century they are usually simple in treatment, with octagonal or circular piers, or perhaps alternating in the same arcade, the arch mouldings in two orders with chamfered edges framed by a weather moulding. Sometimes however an elaboration of mouldings was attempted in imitation of the greater churches, as at Eaton Bray and West Walton. In churches such as Salisbury, Hexham and Southwell this duplication of mouldings forms an integral part of the general scheme, but in a small parish church is entirely out of place; for in this century the small church relied upon proportion for its interest, which was easy to destroy by over elaboration, the voussoirs crowded with mouldings which if not carefully handled became furrowed and stringy, as we see them at Eaton Bray. This over-enrichment was a relic of the preceding age, in which surface decoration was employed to cover poor proportions and bad construction; in the thirteenth century however this palliative was no longer necessary.

The thirteenth century piers in addition to circular and octagonal forms were designed with separate shafts as at Skirbeck, Lincolnshire, where they stand upon a double base. At Dewsbury, Yorkshire and Stone, Kent, the piers are tall and slender, four shafted, one at each of the cardinal points and clamped together by moulded rings similar to Salisbury. At West Walton the piers are shorter with a sturdier core; at Edenham they are a combination of Hartlepool and Dewsbury with variations in the same arcade. The bases are often elaborated with what are called hold-water mouldings; these, although delightful in themselves, especially when applied to a capital, are unpractical and wrong-headed when used in a base for external work, the frost and rain decomposing the stone. The caps are bell-shaped with a fillet or necking below and graceful undercut mouldings above; when unencumbered by foliage carving these caps are extraordinarily happy in their form and apposite in their position.

During this time the main walls of the greater churches were divided above the arcades into triforiums and clerestories, forming a triple-storeyed building divided by horizontal strings (79). This design was not constant however, the triforium varying in importance from the tremendous example in the nave at Ely which challenges the arcade below, to the insignificant triforium in the nave at Tewkesbury. Further a triforium was not a necessity, even in the earlier time, for it was combined with the arcade at St. Frideswides, Oxford, and at Glastonbury, and later with the clerestory in the quires at Pershore and Southwell. The average design gave less importance to the triforium than to either of its partners, but it nevertheless provided a band of decoration where it was needed, forming the connecting link between the other two. The single arch of the Romanesque gave place to two arches to the bay, which was again subdivided into from two to four lights. At Salisbury however the single arch was retained with unhappy results, for it sprawls and appears crushed down by the masonry above it. Another design was a continuous band of arcading as in the nave at Wells, and the quires at Beverley and Southwell; at Chester also both in the quire of the cathedral and the nave of St. John and in the transept at York; this type, effective in itself, tends to stress the horizontality of the layout.

The triple division of the main wall is continued in the fourteenth century in the quires at Lincoln and Ely and in the north

79 CHICHESTER CATHEDRAL, LOOKING EAST

80 LANERCOST NAVE, INTERIOR, THIRTEENTH CENTURY

81 WINCHCOMBE, GLOUCESTERSHIRE, EXTERIOR NAVE, SIXTEENTH CENTURY

transept at Hereford. In the quire at Wells however an elaborate nichework design takes the place of the triforium; in the quires at St. Albans and Exeter (96) the triforium takes a subordinate position; the former continuous, the latter in groups of five set just below the clerestory windows. In the quire at York, the quire at Guisborough, and the south side of the nave at Bridlington, the triforium and clerestory are designed as a single unit, the lower half of the window forming the triforium; in the last-named the elimination is almost complete, and entirely so at Selby, where arcade and clerestory form a satisfactory combination. The disappearance of the triforium in the fourteenth century was a mixed blessing; where the wall space had been well thought out with a large single arch for the arcade, two lesser arches for the triforium and three for the clerestory, it was possible to produce a charmingly proportioned bay as in the quire at Rievaulx (32), or, without the top three, at Lichfield; its abolition nevertheless helped considerably towards unity, for the horizontal line was now replaced by the vertical, and when this idea was fully developed in the fifteenth century it produced a sense of height and dignity that the earlier triple setting out had failed to achieve.

As the ascetic force of the monastic ideal decreased by the close of the thirteenth century, so the architectural outlook changed with it; no longer was it governed by severity, aloofness and height, combined with a certain tendency toward hardness which was continued during the first stages of the geometric style, with its uninspired mechanical compass window tracery. Gradually however architecture became more human in its expression, buildings grew lighter both in the actual weight of masonry and in the size of the windows; the builders, though now content with less ambitious heights, found compensation in breadth, suggesting that churches were communal centres as well as places of worship. The devotion accorded to the B.V.M. had a refining influence, the delicate and lacelike decoration reflecting an almost tender cast of thought.

During the first centuries the fabrics of the parish churches were a simplified reflection of what was taking place in the construction of cathedral and abbey; it was a rare occurrence for a parish church to strike an individual note of its own. The change to the fourteenth century was gradual, for the arcades at Adderbury and Broughton in Oxfordshire and Great Brington in Northamptonshire might almost be classed with the thirteenth century were it not for a certain freedom of handling, the arches wider and more spacious in their outlines. Certain districts were in advance of others although as yet there was little local individuality in style apart from that necessitated by circumstances or dictated by building materials. The average fourteenth century arcade is composed of shafted piers of considerable height; although circular and octagonal forms are found at Cley, Norfolk, and Woodstock, Oxfordshire. More arches are moulded and fewer chamfered, the former at Patrington and Edenham, the latter at Halsall and Claypole. Where piers are shafted they often continue the keel edge, the capitals following the shafting of the piers of four half circles, the mouldings now cut a little deeper, the bell shape however a little narrower. They are delightfully set out at Threckingham and Rippingale in Lincolnshire, Hedon in Yorkshire, Cotton, Suffolk, and Clifton Reynes, Buckinghamshire, this last of almost diamond shape with the corners chamfered away; an arcade combining the finest qualities of both periods.

About the middle of the fourteenth century England was visited by the Black Death brought from the Continent, its rapid progress being the result of a complete lack of sanitation combined with a totally inadequate knowledge of its treatment. This scourge, thrice repeated owing to the carelessness and the hopeless resignation of the people, swept through the land, taking toll of the educated and intelligent and leaving masons' yards, vicarages, monasteries and farms untenanted and derelict, sapping the vitality and manhood of the race and leaving the country exhausted. From this unparalleled disaster England was long in recovering, for the flower and beauty, the gay chivalry and pageantry of the early fourteenth century had been crushed. When the country stirred again the minds of the people were fixed on the uncertainty of life and the necessity of insuring their souls while there was yet time; hence the popularity of prayers for the dead and the new-found interest in the parish church. Neither monastery nor cathedral was concerned in the salvation of the common people; the friars however won golden opinions by their courage in visiting and ministering to the plague-stricken people. The plague had its repercussions in the masons' yards, where there were insufficient men available for the work required, made worse at times by the impressment of masons for the king's works.

However, from the less stricken Severn Valley a new mode of building was already at hand, for the masons there had been confronted with the problem of rehabilitating the old massive heavy twelfth century abbey church at Gloucester, and bringing it up to the standard of taste and skill then prevailing, without however incurring the enormous cost of pulling down the church and rebuilding it. This had been made possible by the

83 LICHFIELD, LADY CHAPEL

82 NORWICH CATHEDRAL, EAST END

TWELFTH AND FIFTEENTH CENTURY WALL ARCADES

courage and foresight of Abbot Thokey who had found sanctuary for the murdered and cast out body of Edward II. Later
his shrine became immensely popular and the abbey church
was to be re-modelled in his honour from the contributions of
the faithful. The new style was first tried out in the south transept, 1329–1337 (10), and was accomplished by the insertion of
larger windows and by a system of refacing the interior walls
with stone panelling with vertical and horizontal mouldings
irrespective of what stood behind; it proved so successful that
it was later applied to the quire and presbytery with the addition
of a magnificent clerestory and lierne vault[1] (99). Earlier than
this work at Gloucester however the new approach to building
methods may be seen in the quire of the abbey of St. Augustine
at Bristol undertaken during the abbacy of Knowles 1306–1332.
This remarkable building is a foretaste of things to come,
incredibly in advance of its time; the aisles carried up to the
height of the quire, abolishing both triforium and clerestory;
the exterior in many ways resembling that of a fifteenth century
college chapel with fine high windows placed between noble
buttressing.

With this new method stone could be cut and finished at the
quarry centres ready for fixing, and this was made necessary by
the dearth of masons; however what at first had been obligatory
later became more or less the normal procedure in so far as
ashlar-faced cutting was involved. Scientific building was sufficiently advanced to guide the thrusts of a vault through its ribs
to given points where buttressing took the weight of the vaulting. This enabled the builder to eliminate the wall veil and
provide as much window space as was required for the now
popular stained glass. When an existing church was remodelled,
the aisle walls were heightened to produce larger and more
spacious windows; in addition a second series was erected
above the arcades, forming an almost continuous clerestory. As
the earlier arcades were now too low to do justice to the new
aisle windowing, they were removed, otherwise there would be
an unsightly surface of plain walling between the arcade and
the clerestory, spoiling the proportions of the church, as at
Great Malvern. In innumerable instances arcades were re-

[1] The ridiculous attitude of Victorians to the last phase of mediaeval
architecture is well shown by the remark of Professor Freeman "the quire
paid for by the offerings at Edward II shrine . . . to that abnormal worship
the abbey owes its present form. I am half inclined to put it the other way,
and to make a new count in the articles of deposition against the unworthy
king that this misguided devotion has cost us the abbey of Serlo in its
perfect form, and hinders us from studying the contrast which we should
otherwise have been able to mark between its eastern and its western limb."

K

designed and the churches became a framework in stone for a coloured lantern in glass, wonderfully light, airy, and graceful; this new direction was often combined with the revival of an earlier building plan, a church without structural division between nave and chancel which was admirably realized in many town churches.

This last phase of mediaeval architecture was exactly suited to the parish church, much more effective than the remodelling of great twelfth century buildings, and this is as it should be, for the days of abbeys were drawing to a close, whereas the parish church was coming into its own. Bath Abbey does not fill one with admiration, for it lacks its mediaeval setting of glass and furniture. The style unfortunately suffers for its merits, for when the treasures for which a church was built have been wantonly destroyed it leaves an aching void. In the greater buildings the quire at Winchester is good straightforward building of arcade and clerestory (77, 123), light strong, well-proportioned and with little waste of material. The refacing of the nave and also the quire at Gloucester are both ingenious and successful. The impossibility of removing the masses of masonry of the twelfth century and rebuilding from the ground has been overcome by a new surface and remodelling; in both examples the horizontality of three divisions has disappeared—the shafts reach without a break from the ground to the vault, producing a sense of height and stateliness which in the early periods was unknown; the new clerestories, completed above by lierne vaulting, give a splendid finish to a clever scheme of transmutation. At Sherborne the same methods were applied, but here the fan vault (102) is entirely relevant to the panelling, continuing the scheme without a visible break; in all these refacings of earlier masonry, stone panelling takes an important place, as it also does in new erections as at St. Mary Redcliff.

In the new work of parish church construction octagonal piers and chamfered arches were continued, as at Terrington and Knowle. At Church Handborough, Oxfordshire and Northleach, Gloucestershire (85), the facets of the piers are hollowed slightly, the capping following the same curves. The clustered piers with four half shafts and connected caps are at Thirsk (91) with moulded arches, and at Skipton with chamfered ones; in Devon clustered piers composed of many small members with foliaged caps are general, as at Bradninch, Kenton and Tor Bryan, combined with elaborately moulded arcades. Another and earlier type is the glorious nave arcades of Hull Holy Trinity, with slender tall piers and acutely pointed arches; this

87 BEVERLEY ST. MARY, EAST

86 DURHAM, SOUTH AISLE, WEST

89 KIRKBY LONSDALE, TWELFTH CENTURY

88 LONG MELFORD, SUFFOLK, FIFTEENTH CENTURY

was continued at Holbeach, Lincolnshire, and was completed at Cirencester; here the piers have six slender shafts with diminutive caps and bases, between which the hollow of the pier is carried through to the apex of the arch. There are many varieties of this type as at Chulmleigh, Devon, Banwell, Somerset, Bunbury, Cheshire and Norwich St. Giles.

The beautiful arcades at Tattershall (92) and at Cirencester takes note of the introduction of pewing, the base mouldings rising well above it. During this period there was also a growing tendency to dispense with capitals, either moulded or carved; this is half accomplished at Great Gransden, Huntingdonshire and wholly so at Harewood, Wintringham and St. Martin le Grand, York (now blitzed). An intermediate type has the arches and piers panelled as in the north chapel at St. Cuthbert, Wells, and in the refacing of the nave arcades at Sherborne. In the end the four-centred arch was depressed, forming a Tudor shape as at Winchcombe and Northleach, Gloucestershire (85), Hemingborough, Yorkshire, in several churches in North Wales as well as Cheshire. This arch realized the earlier endeavours and is an answer to any question as to the continuity and progress in masoncraft and design.

In both monastic and secular churches the clerestory was from the first the third member of the triple design, and the only means of lighting a nave apart from the west window. The windows were however spaced widely apart and set within an interior arcade fencing a narrow footway tunnelled through the wall and used in case of repairs. Building progress in the twelfth century was quite inadequate to take advantage of the possibilities offered by this method of lighting; they had to be content with spare windowing, which was expensive enough to glaze at the time.

In the early parish churches clerestory lighting was unusual, although occasionally found, as at Frodsham, where it is however much restored. At Whaplode, Lincolnshire, and St. Margaret-at-Cliffe, Kent, arcading is made the feature of the exterior, a round-headed window placed in every third or fourth arch. Circular windows are used in the nave at Southwell, one to each bay, fenced within by a round-headed arcade. The thirteenth century continued the same approach, the windowing often set in an arcade; on the exterior at Darlington and both at West Walton. A charming feature in the interior of the nave at Lanercost is the delicately moulded continuous arcade protecting the clerestory; this is repeated in the transepts at Hedon. At Hexham and elsewhere the triple arcade in each bay gives an essential importance to the top storey. In the parish church the usual method was to place a number of lancets unconnected in design with each other either within or without as at Elm, Cambridgeshire. A typical church at Haltwhistle, Northumberland has but three small single lancets forming the clerestory to the nave, for it was not until the fourteenth century that any real use of the clerestory for lighting was made and then it was sporadic. In the naves of Pembridge and Hunstanton four small circular windows are used; the collegiate nave at Howden has small doubled lights at intervals; however at Cley in Norfolk large circular windows alternate with pointed ones crowded along the clerestory in picturesque disarray. No particular development in the greater churches took place during the fourteenth century; in the nave at Lichfield and north transept at Hereford a curious spherical triangle is employed, quite beautiful and matching the curved lines of the vaulting on either side.

Clerestories in parish churches were never common even in the fifteenth and sixteenth centuries. They are rare in the southwest, almost absent in Wales, and Southern counties can boast of few. In other parts they are, with certain exceptions, of quite ordinary type, possibly larger in size than the preceding period, but still unconnected with the arcade below even when they formed part of the exterior design. The clerestory was, however, brought to great perfection in many town churches as St. Stephen, Norwich, and St. Mary, Bury St. Edmunds, especially where the plan of a through church had been fully carried out. In East Anglia, Lincolnshire, Warwickshire, and in the north in Yorkshire, Nottinghamshire, Staffordshire and Cheshire are many fine examples of clerestories with almost continuous windowing. This fine addition to a church produced both nobility and height; it was moreover light and spacious, successfully challenging the great churches in impressiveness and beauty, and when these splendidly proportioned windows were filled with contemporary glass, the effect must have been magnificent.

With a clerestory of this description a thrusting roof was constructionally unsound, for the walls were unsupported and too thin to rebut the weight against them; to eliminate this difficulty a beam roof was employed of sufficient camber to give the required pitch to the lead flats above to throw off the rain. On the inside, the roof was either panelled, as ornate or simple as desired, or left raftered, usually, however, painted and gilt, catching the reflected light from the clerestory windows. Outside, the new clerestory gave a second line of windowing to the façade, which, combined with the pinnacled parapets, compensated for the loss of the sky line shown by the earlier high-pitched roof.

The arrangement and shape of the heads of the clerestory windows varied considerably; they were four-centred as at St. Mary Redcliff (6), straight sided as at Terrington St. Clement, square headed as at Winchcombe (81), and in breadth from one to four lights, placed singly, in pairs or continuous sequence, with or without narrow buttressing. These windows are usually shorter than those of the aisles, but are proportionate and dignified in scale, set well back from the exterior edge to give the appearance of strength combined with light and shade. Splendid examples of this interesting phase of the fifteenth and sixteenth centuries are to be found in East Anglia at Blythburgh, Lavenham, Long Melford (88) and Southwold; the Lavenham set with continuous three-light windowing surmounted by an elaborately carved openwork parapet.[1]

The greater churches had a unified design for the main inner walls from the twelfth century; such a scheme however was not introduced into the parish church until well into the fifteenth century. In the meanwhile frescoes were painted upon the walls; at Astbury the wall between arcade and clerestory is set out in moulded oblong panels in which may be seen traces of painting. However, the Severn Valley system of panelled decoration is used with excellent results, the spacing between arcade and window being filled in several ways. This is shown in its completeness at St. Mary Redcliff, Lavenham, Long Melford (88) and Saffron Waldon. It is also used for filling the spandrels above the arcade at Beverley St. Mary (87), Mold and Bebington. At Northleach (85), Cirencester and Tattershall (92) the connection is made by framing the window by shafts from the pier caps to the roof line; at Tickhill by ogee finialed mouldings above the arches; at Southam, although there is no real connection, the clerestory cills by means of tracery have been brought down to the top level of the arcades. At St. Mary Redcliff the panelling is applied to the exterior walls of the clerestory both of nave and chancel (6). On odd occasions where an aisle had not been erected, the second tier of windows was continued in the straight wall as at Ditcheat, Somerset, and Long Itchington, Warwickshire.

[1] In Lincolnshire at Tattershall, Billingborough and two sets at Burgh. In Gloucestershire at Chipping Campden, Cirencester, and Northleach. In Warwickshire at Southam; Staffordshire, Gnosall; Salop, Newtown; Yorkshire, Thirsk (91), Tickhill and Beverley St. Mary (87). In Lancashire at Sephton, and Standish and in Cheshire at Astbury, Audlem, Barthomley, Brereton and Nantwich.

THE PROTECTION FROM THE ELEMENTS. FIRE AND WATER

A VERY real and ever present dread in mediæval times was the fear of fire, which, owing to the plentiful use of timber with no adequate means of fighting the flames, was a constant danger to the inhabitants of monasteries, cathedrals and dwelling-houses. The history of many an important church gives an account of devastating fires, interspersed by the disasters of falling towers, caused through miscalculation or insecure foundations. It was indeed a laborious road the early builders had to travel before anything approaching immunity from either could in any way be assured. The vivid description given by the monk Gervase in 1174, of the destruction by fire of Canterbury Cathedral, is filled with the anguish caused by the desolation and extinction of the labours of many years.

The urgent problem was therefore to eliminate the cause, and for the future to safeguard the buildings from further disasters. As a timber roof was the most inflammable part of the church, an inner protection of stonework was devised and applied when feasible. Unfortunately, at the close of the eleventh and beginning of the twelfth centuries, builders were still making use of the tunnel, domical, or groined vault of Roman origin; a vault rigid in setting out, incapable of alteration in form, and both weighty and inert. One of these several forms was in regular use for the protection of aisles, but was too clumsy and heavy for a high vault; it was tried more than once, usually ending in failure. The quire of Durham was so vaulted in 1104, but by 1235 an indulgence states that the stone vault of the quire was then a threatening ruin. The earliest remaining high vaults of this period are those placed over the transepts of the same church, which Dr. John Bilson dates about 1110. These early attempts of covering a large space with a stone vault were very primitive, for the Roman methods had been lost.

The Normans used a transverse arch to divide up their vaulting into bays and to form a centring for the groining which was composed principally of rubble with quantities of cement, which when set became a solid mass, having little thrust but unduly heavy both to support and carry. This type of groined vault may be seen in the crypts of Lastingham, Yorkshire, 1078–1088; Winchester and St. Peter-in-the-East, Oxford (94);

90 RIPON, QUIRE, LOOKING EAST

FIFTEENTH CENTURY ARCADE DESIGN

91 THIRSK, YORKSHIRE, NAVE, LOOKING WEST

92 TATTERSHALL, NORTH NAVE ARCADE

also the north aisle at Blyth, the nave aisles at Ely, the Gloucester ambulatory, Winchester transepts and at St. Bartholomew,
Smithfield (78); this last however was not begun before 1123.
The aisle bays are generally square in shape, formed by bi-
secting two tunnels or half circles at right angles, leaving the
arrises or groins roughly cemented. This early type was homogeneous with the walls it covered, the half circle of the transverse arches matched against either wall, the inside one following the line of the round-headed arch of the arcade, the outer
that of the window; this constructional unity was not again in
late ages so closely achieved.

High vaults were never self-supporting even when placed
upon thick Norman walling, but required abutment to resist
their weight and thrust. At Durham this took the form of
internal flying buttresses placed under the roofs of the aisles,
that of the quire 1093–1096 forming a complete arch, that in the
nave 1099–1128 a segment of a circle; both forms however
conveyed some of the thrust from the clerestory to the walls of
the aisles. These internal buttresses are constructionally sound,
completely protected as they are from the elements; later when
churches took an increasing height they were taken outside, a
type of stone scaffold where they require watchful repair.

An important advance was made in vaulting construction by
the addition of diagonal ribs springing from each corner and
crossing at the centre. This was a good move, for the framework
could be first erected and the webbing filled in later, the ribs
also conveyed the thrust of the vault down to the corners. This
type is used in the transepts at Durham and is also found in the
majority of the aisles of the same building. It also appears in the
nave aisles of Southwell, Gloucester, Malmesbury and Selby.
During this time vaulting in parish churches was confined to
chancels, sanctuaries, porches and crypts. The chancels at
Stow, Lincolnshire, Rudford (95), Elkstone and Hampnett in
Gloucestershire, and at Hemel Hempstead are treated in this
way, as are St. Mary and St. John, Devizes, the sanctuary at
Kilpeck, a chapel at Tewkesbury and a crypt at Berkswell. The
Elkstone vault shows the beginnings of the central boss, for the
ribs are carved with dragons' heads where they cross. Sometimes
a ridge rib was added, and this was as far as it was possible to
take the quadripartite vault based upon the round arch, which
in its setting out and construction was incapable of further
development.

At this time the pointed arch, already in use as decoration,
began to be used constructionally; it solved the difficulty of
fitting a vault to any given space while keeping an even keel,

which seems to have been a tenet of the period. Tentatively used at first, it is illustrated by our finest early example in the nave vault at Durham, 1128–1133 (93), where the great transverse arches are pointed, lifting the vault to a new height; the later quire vault, 1278, follows the same setting out as does the quadripartite vault of the nine altars. The vaulting of this wonderful building is stressed, for it is essentially one of the most important series of examples to be found in Europe.

The advantage of this new system was striking, for it was no longer essential to support the whole of a bay during construction; each section could be erected independently and so long as the foundations held good there was a minimum risk of collapse; lesser spaces were easier to fill and the ribs with their decorative mouldings became pleasant features of the building. During the first quarter of the twelfth century chevron ornament is applied prodigally to vaulting ribs as it was to chancel arches, doorways and wall arcades; Durham is an outstanding example of this treatment; the nave and south transept vaults, triforium arcades and the Galilee arches (7) are encrusted with it, the last with three rows. The simple ribbed quadripartite vault of this date is the foundation upon which all the further developments both in shape and intricacy have been built; appearances might change, but the elements remain constant (86).

In shape the earlier ribs are square and strong with a fillet running along each edge, and they are constructed with small voussoirs; the transverse arches were wide and stout, capable of withstanding considerable weight and rebutting thrusts; when however the masons had grown accustomed to the new principles they found it reasonable to thin down both without in any way interfering with their constructional quality; ribs ceased to be square, they became narrow and chamfered, the transverse arch reduced to an ordinary rib, both in size and shape. In the majority of the early thirteenth century vaults the ridge rib is omitted 79); and this is not disadvantageous for there seems to have been some difficulty in keeping a straight line, noticeable in the quire aisles at Southwell where each section of the ridge slightly changes its direction. In the following set of examples the ridge rib is omitted; in Boxgrove quire, the transverse arch is still predominant; in the vaults at Salisbury, nave, aisles and cloisters, New Shoreham quire, and Blyth nave all the ribs are of equal dimensions. Parish churches continued to have occasional vaults in the chancels, at Broadwater, Bishop's Cannings, Easton, Hampshire and Gloucester St. Mary de Lode; but vaulting continued to be the exception.

In the new methods a difficulty arose at the crossing of the

93 DURHAM NAVE; WALLS 1093–96, VAULT 1128–33

TWELFTH CENTURY VAULTING

GROIN VAULTING

QUADRIPARTITE VAULTING

ribs, for it is neither easy nor structurally sound to scribe the ribs to fit where they meet; this was surmounted by adopting a keystone, first of small size as at Salisbury, Blyth and Broadwater, where the ribs butt into a small solid stone cut to shape to meet their contact. The keystone became an important point of interest, it was gradually enlarged and enriched, the quire at Southwell providing exquisite examples of trefoil foliage carving. It would appear to have been a matter of complete indifference to the carvers whether their work could be studied or not; this did not prevent them from enjoying their labours and cutting some excellent and lovely work, which today we can examine through binoculars. Keystones served a further purpose, for if sufficiently heavy they kept the vaulting ribs in place for they are liable to spring; central keystones weigh anything up to a couple of tons and later they play a vital part in vault design.

Masons were however not long content with a simple quadripartite vault, for they realized the decorative qualities of the rib and proceeded to multiply their numbers until at Exeter (96) eleven ribs spring from each diagonal point, providing a soaring and splendid finish to a glorious building. This occasioned another problem, that of springing a number of ribs from a small half-round cap. As this was a sheer impossibility a further constructional improvement was effected by bonding the springers into the wall and projecting them horizontally to a height from which the ribs could be conveniently arcuated; this ensured the anchoring of vault to wall.

With the use of the tierceron rib system as at Exeter (96), that is ribs which spring from a diagonal point and meet the ridge but not of necessity at the actual crossing, a cross ridge in addition to the main ridge rib was an essential. This cross ridge is placed across the centre of a bay and extends from window to window; both cross ridge and main ridge are kept horizontal and on the same plane. This cross rib must not be confounded with the transverse arched rib whose work was the dividing of the vaulting into bays. Constructionally the cross rib is by no means uniform; it may be taken straight across the vault as in the quire at Ely, or stopped part way as in the presbytery of the same building; or it could be tipped upwards above the head of the windows before it reached the wall as at Winchester. The blocking out of the light coming through the clerestory windows by the spring of the vault had also to be met; this was by no means easy, especially if the vault sprang from the base of the clerestory or even below it; when however the spring was taken from half way up the clerestory wall this difficulty seldom

L

occurred. It was solved in different ways: at Winchester by tipping up the vault pocket above the window, at Southwell by plough-sharing the ribs and webbing on either side of the window, that is, by forcing and pressing back and preventing them following their correct radius. If the curve of the rib remained undisturbed this subterfuge would pass unnoticed from below.

The tierceron form of vaulting in addition to decoration provided an easier method of filling in the webbing by breaking up the large spaces to be covered. In England rubble was used, and though cheaper than ashlar was heavier, hardly less ever than a foot in thickness, and therefore required stronger abutment. The French owing to the height and breadth of their ambitious churches had been compelled earlier to find a way of reducing the weight of their vaults, and had accomplished this by filling the webbing with thin ashlar slabs rabbetted to the ribs. The English however, although they copied this method now and then especially in the south, continued the use of rubble for their main filling. Up to the time when the quadripartite vault in England was changing its form the French were the more accomplished craftsmen in the erection of vaults; they however were quite satisfied with their formula and ceased to explore further possibilities. Fortunately the English continued their experiments until at the close of the mediaeval period we could show a magnificent series of tierceron, lierne and fan vaults.

Perhaps tierceron vaulting shows itself to greater perfection over the polygonal chapter-houses of our cathedrals and monasteries, at Westminster, Lincoln, Margam, Salisbury and Wells (97). The majority had a central pillar to support the vault, but the Yorkshire masons, ever venturesome, constructed York and Southwell without. Chapter-houses with a central pillar have tierceron ribs on the outer half of the circle, met on the inner side by straight ribs as at Westminster and Margam. At Wells (97) the tiercerons are met on the inner side by thirty-two ribs which die into the capping of the pier. The unsupported vaults at York and Southwell are constructed with transverse arches, cross ridges and tiercerons; the latter meet at the ridging; both these examples are of extreme delicacy and richness.

An unusual type is a double vault, where the transverse and diagonal ribs are shadowed below with skeleton ribs springing from a lower point, as in the chancel of St. Mary, Warwick, St. Augustine, Bristol and St. Davids both by Bristol masons. Parish churches show little vaulting outside towers and porches;

96   EXETER, LOOKING WEST, FOURTEENTH CENTURY

FAN VAULTING

TIERCERON VAULTING

chapels and aisles were however to come later. The simply designed tower vaults of Bleadon and Wellow with the curious example at Norton St. Philip, all in Somerset; the central tower vault at Minster Lovel, Oxfordshire, and the octagon porch at Redcliff, are good examples of parish church masoncraft.

A further development in vaulting design soon appeared known as lierne vaulting. Up to this point the rib had always been constructional, but it was now to become a decoration as well; indeed, its functional use gradually declined until it lost much of its organic meaning and was often reduced to the position of surface ornament. The lierne vault is so called on account of the use of numbers of short ribs connecting one point with another, arranged in designs which are capable of infinite variety. The ribs are set out in squares, Maltese crosses and diamonds, all featured at Redcliff; star-shaped in the quires of St. Augustine, Bristol, and the lovely examples at Tewkesbury and Ely. Other elaborate designs are in the presbytery at Norwich, Nantwich chancel, the Lady chapel at Ely, and the nave of Redcliff. The north transept at Gloucester has a vault without bosses, the intersections of the ribs carefully scribed.

In the later vaults voussoirs of the ribs are lengthened; it was found that in this form they were constructionally stronger; in these later types of vaulting design the central ridge rib is essential sometimes in triplicate, as at Gloucester (99) in the quire, the north transept, the Lady chapel and at the west end of the nave, also in Tewkesbury nave and Redcliff quire. In the greater churches charming designs are used for tower vaulting at York, Lincoln and Tewkesbury; in lesser churches at Cricklade, Redcliff, St. Nicholas, Gloucester, and Winscombe, Somerset. Tower vaults always include a large central circular well for hoisting and lowering bells. Porches are enriched in the same charming manner, as at Woolpit, Suffolk; it is however impossible to list the many varieties both of design and detail.

A startling departure is made in the quire vaults at Gloucester (99) and Ottery St. Mary, a throwback to an earlier age, for these vaults are constructed on the principle of a barrel enriched with ribs whose purpose is that of decoration. The thrust is kept down by the steepness of the curve, for the steeper the curve the lesser the thrust. These extraordinary vaults are not supported by flying buttresses, and at Gloucester the earlier internal ones do little to assist the new high vault.

It was not a great step from lierne to fan, and several lierne vaults show the use of conoids in the construction. They appear in the vaults of the Divinity school (100) and St. Frideswides (now the cathedral) (101), Oxford and in more complete form at Sherborne (102). Transverse arches are again prominent, giving support to this new form of construction. Transitional periods often produce the more interesting architectural work, such as from twelfth to thirteenth century, and from mediaeval to classic. The same flair appears in vault design from lierne to fan, it would indeed be difficult to name three vaults of greater charm than those just given, perhaps the premier place should be given to St. Frideswides (Oxford Cathedral), 1500 (101). Here the vault has been narrowed on either side by a band of barrel vaulting and only commences half-way up the transverse arches; from these conoids are developed with pendant lanterns; the lierne ribs of the centre space producing a lovely stellar design. The elongated boss or pendant is at this time a feature of vault construction, either as a centre, or a finish to a conoid.

The vault of the Divinity school (100) is low, owing to the library above and is not more than twenty feet from the ground and may therefore be examined in detail. The arches are flattened, matching the heads of the windows, the conoids placed on either side the transverse arches having pendants with small niches containing figures of the doctors of the church; the vault crowded with heraldic bosses, badges and designs. This vault was commenced in 1424, but owing to financial difficulties was not completed until after 1480. Other examples of this time are at Christchurch, Twynham, and St. George's, Windsor (129). In the former, 1502–1520, vaulting starts from the transverse arch and not from the springer, forming conoids with pendants, lierne ribs forming stellar ornament in the centre of each bay. In the quire of St. George's, 1505–1520 the pendants are in the centre; this curious design falls into three parts, lierne vaulting on either side with panelling in the centre. The transverse arch forms the centring but not where the diagonals cross. The panelled centre is another example of triple ridging, with six pointed stars with pendants surrounded by quatrefoils.

The essential difference between a lierne and a fan vault lies in the rib (119); in the former each rib has a different curve and length, in the latter the ribs are alike in curve, length and spacing; this lightened the labour in setting out but complicated it in other directions. It is a form equally successful either in miniature placed over a tomb, or sufficiently great to cover the quire of an abbey church. It may be constructed with an ashlar filling, or formed by stone panels with the ribs actually cut upon them; it is always kept thin and light to prevent thrust.

The fan vault was a fitting crown to the work of the Severn Valley school of masons and is their greatest triumph; in a way it is the apotheosis of our mediaeval period, an English development uninfluenced from abroad, for the Gloucester masons took a leading role during the last phase. Both in its setting out and detail the fan vault is in the closest connection with their constructional planning, both in the shape of their arches, mouldings, and the panelling of the walls. It moreover followed the sound principle that the eye should be led upwards to the more excellent features just as in tower design the belfry stage is the chief point of interest.

Although many examples remain, others have perished; we would like to know what developments were shown in the destroyed abbeys of Cirencester, Evesham and Winchcombe? Tewkesbury had similar cloisters to Gloucester (98), and the vault over the north aisle at Cirencester probably came from elsewhere. Of greater examples there are Sherborne (102) and Bath abbeys, King's College chapel (125) and the unsurpassed and glorious example over the chapel of Henry VII at Westminster (126). Lesser vaults include the aisles at Bath, Sherborne and Windsor, with the crossing at the latter and the north transept at Sherborne; the chapels at Ottery and Cullompton and the cloisters at Gloucester (98), together with a fair number of small vaults over chapels, porches and towers.

Fan vaults may be placed in three divisions; first where the conoids do not meet across the ridge; secondly where they meet but do not overlap at the sides; and thirdly where they overlap either at the sides or crossing; the last two need certain qualifications, and there are minor types here and there. Sherborne (102) is the outstanding example of the first type; if it be judged by the rule of equal ribs in curve and distance then it is a true fan vault; both nave and quire are the same type, the conoids doubling their panelled tracery as they curve upwards; the lierne planning has however not been abandoned, for the ridge, cross-ridge and diagonals are still in evidence with a happy patterning of lierne ribs placed between the conoids down the centre of the vault. Both these vaults are lovely; that of the quire flatter owing to constructional difficulties, but the more successful in that the vaulting shafts spring from the ground instead of above the arcade as in the nave; later fan vaults are perhaps more logical, but none more delightful, rich and satisfying.

Where the conoids meet but do not overlap as in the second type, a fairly large flat panel is left in the centres between them, which is only possible when the vault is small as in the aisles of

Henry VII's chapel, Westminster, with pendants, and Windsor chapel without; Gloucester cloisters have eight quatrefoils in the space (98); Cirencester aisle and porch, All Saints, Evesham, Wilcot chapel, North Leigh, with four; Evesham St. Lawrence and the Vernon chapel, Tong, Salop, with pendants, and the towers of Milton Abbas, Mells and Axbridge with open bell holes. The design is usually excellent, avoiding too much flat panelling to negotiate between the conoids.

The third type includes the greater vaults over the chapel of Henry VII at Westminster, King's College chapel and Bath abbey as well as the aisle chapels at Ottery and Cullompton and such tiny specimens as that over the Poyntz chapel, St. Mark's, Bristol. Only at Ottery and the aisles of Bath do the conoids cut across each other at the ridge; the others however are shorn off at the sides, not too happy at Bath and distinctly unpleasant at King's College, Cambridge (125), where the transverse arches are given undue prominence. What shall be said however of the magnificent vault over the chapel of Henry VII at Westminster?, without exaggeration one of the wonders of mediaeval architecture, a vault which to the eye seems suspended in mid-air, encrusted as it is with perforated ornament of the most delicate description, with no hard lines or misshapen features (126). The conoids with pendants are constructed upon the transverse arches, the conoids intersecting and the vault kept high at the sides, the pendants repeated in the centre panels of the vault. The apsidal east end, separated by a wide transverse arch, is achieved by an outside circle of conoids enclosing a stellar panel blazoned with badges. This vault gives to us a knowledge that even if the Suppression had not taken place, the ingenuity of the masons could not have bettered this marvellous example of constructive craftsmanship.

The traceried panelling used for the decoration of the conoids is admirable; no other treatment *was* possible when the principle was grasped; it is worked out with two or three expanding rings or storeys, each one as the upward curve expands duplicating the one below; this prevents overcrowding at the base and paucity above. At the first break many of these designs are carved with delightful forms of ogee tracery, the mullions of the lower stage continuing with the addition of a second series springing from the tips of the ogees; this second order is completed by quatrefoils above the tracery heads. Although it may be thought that fan vaults are of a similar design, that is not so, and the variety displayed would engage the attention of the curious observer for some little time.

Although a stone vault may seal a building from above, it

99 GLOUCESTER, QUIRE, VAULT

100 DIVINITY SCHOOL, OXFORD

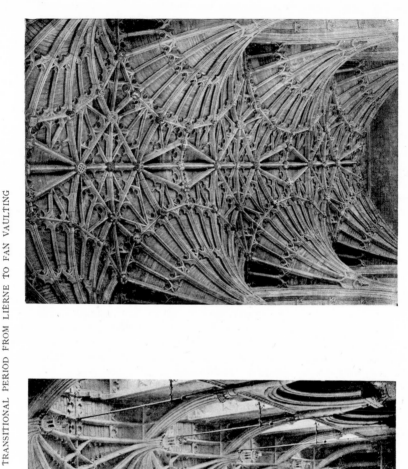

102 SHERBORNE ABBEY, NAVE, DORSET

101 ST. FRIDESWIDE, QUIRE, OXFORD

still requires a timber roof to protect it from the elements, for the upper side of a vault is usually humpbacked and clumsy, with deep pockets at regular intervals against the walls, the vault covered with a thick layer of cement. The pitch of the outer roof varied according to period; the Normans usually at an angle of 45 degrees, the thirteenth century as much as 60, and the sixteenth century as low as 10. The space between the vault and the outer roof is generally lit by a window in the gable of the building, and the space is largely filled with the timber scaffolding upholding the outer roof. The average type has strong baulks of timber bridging over the vault and resting upon the outer walls; into these are mortised and tenoned the principals or frames which are supported by a kingpost, possible queen posts and additional strutting as required. On the frames purlins are placed reaching from one frame to the next, bearing up the stout rafters which form a bed for the heavy lead without. The majority of churches however had no stone vaulting on them, and then something less rough and more sightly was required from the carpenters.

Before describing the various types and the methods employed in the construction of timber roofs, it is apposite to mention timber vaults. These have received condemnation on account of the imitation of one material in another; this is of course a matter of taste; they nevertheless have a grave defect, for instead of protecting a church from fire as did a stone vault, they are an added danger, exemplified in the destruction of York Cathedral and Selby Abbey, when the timber vaults added fuel to the inferno. Perhaps the earliest example is at Warmington, Northamptonshire, dating from the thirteenth century and with little but its age to recommend it. Many of the greater churches were vaulted in timber in place of stone either on account of the instability of the walls or possibly finance, seldom from choice; a variety of types exist: quadripartite over the quires of St. Albans and Ripon, tierceron at Selby, and lierne over the quires of York and Winchester. The carved bosses at Ripon and Winchester are notable; Ripon carved with subjects, while the Winchester vault has a series of sacred emblems and heraldry. The vault over the lantern at Ely of the fourteenth century although now largely renewed, is structurally perhaps the most important example of timberwork in England; it is a tierceron vault surrounding the central octagonal lantern and a triumph of carpenters' craftsmanship both in its construction and design. Other timber vaults remain over the cloisters at Lincoln and the towers of St. David's and Ludlow; but the true function of timber was not an imitation of stone, however clever, but the natural development of its own constituent elements; the carpenters of the fifteenth and sixteenth centuries recognized this and produced splendid results both in form and design. The earlier method of imitation continued until the mid-fourteenth century and was in greater evidence in the making of screens and window tracery than in roofs, where the setting out required some recognition of the nature of timber; for instance that of the tendinous strength latent in the grain of a beam of oak, which enabled it to bridge over considerable spans and retain resilience while bearing a heavy weight.

Mediaeval roof design may be divided into three types, beam roofs (111), trussed roofs (105) and thrusting roofs (104). All three were employed throughout the entire period and were not a gradual evolution of form. A roof constructed with a single pair of rafters independent of each other and suitable only for small spans is called a single-framed roof. If the church was of any width it was necessary to place horizontal timbers beneath the rafters called purlins to support the weight of the roofing materials; these purlins rested upon strong frames or principals placed at regular intervals bridging the width of the church. If the church was not wide a ridge purlin and one half-way down the slope would suffice; if wide, however, two or three purlins were necessary, placed at equal distances. The purlins and wall-plates conveyed the strain from the common rafters to the principals; these were placed either where the wall was best able to bear the strain, that is, between the windows or above the apex of the arches; when roofs are so constructed they are termed double-framed.

The beam roof is an almost flat roof constructed by placing beams at regular intervals across the width of the church (111). The beams are either naturally cambered or cut to this shape to prevent sagging, or they are fitted above by means of tapering pieces to raise them to the required slope. Beams act as a dead weight upon the walls and exert no outward thrust, they are particularly suitable for high clerestories or thin walling. In addition to resting upon the walls the beams are usually strengthened by wall-posts and braces which are curved inwards towards the centres of the beams as at Attleborough, Norfolk. This serves the dual purpose of carrying the weight down the wall where it is strongest and secures the beams when the ends resting upon the walls become decayed, as so constructed in the nave at Ewelme, Oxfordshire. Different means were employed to produce the slope required for the outside roof; either the ridge-purlin was laid on the beam and the side purlins mortised into it, or they were laid on the beam, the ridge purlin raised upon a short post. The decoration of beam roofs was largely confined to moulded beams and carving the face sides of the beams, also the decoration of the wall-plates. Rafters were often left exposed, they are to be seen at Blythburgh, Suffolk, and St. Neots, Huntingdonshire, where they are placed flatways and not on edge as is the modern practice; Blythburgh is further decorated with painted monograms and carved angels. Another scheme is to divide the roof into square panels with moulded sides and carved bosses at the intersections (112), producing an effective and noble finish to a church, a distinctive feature of many roofs in Cheshire at Astbury, Barthomley and Malpas.

The tie-beam or trussed roof belongs to the double-framed type, and if properly designed exerts no outward thrust upon the walls. It is not possible to truss a timber roof without the aid of a tie-beam or a pair of scissor beams, and in England the latter are rare. The constructional varieties of the tie-beams may be divided into three, the couple-close, the queen post (105), and the king-post (109); the queen post is a development of the couple-close roof, and the king-post of the beam roof. When a roof consists of a pair of rafters pitched against each other with their feet framed into a tie-beam it is a couple-close roof. If the principal rafters of the frame are supported by two posts placed on the beam under where the side purlins rest it is a queen-post. If the rafters are supported by a central post from the beam to the apex it is a king-post (109); the former may be seen at Addlethorpe, Lincolnshire (105), and the latter over the nave at Barking, Suffolk. The tie-beam is supported as in the beam roof with wall-posts and arch-braces springing from them. The tie-beam and beam roof are sometimes combined to produce a delightful hybrid, belonging to either estate according to the pitch of the roof. In a group in Somerset these are admirably combined, Ditcheat, Leigh-on-Mendip, Long Sutton, Wellow and St. Cuthbert, Wells, may all be considered beam roofs, while High Ham (109) and Martock (110) are certainly king-post roofs. They have many things in common especially in their decoration, the beams have small squared flowers in one or two rows, the space between the beam and the ridge filled in with carved open tracery panels, and they have their apportioned number of demi-angels bearing shields. Of these examples four are raftered and three panelled; a comparison between the early Barking and the later Martock well shows the development of the carpenters' and carvers' art in the construction and decoration of roofs.

M

Thrusting roofs may be divided into couple roofs, arch-braced, collar and trussed-rafter, and hammer-beam roofs. The thrusting roof placed all its weight against the walls, pushing them outwards, and in its simple form consists of two rafters pitched against each other with their feet resting upon the walls; this is called a couple roof, and only the strength of the walls to resist the pressure prevents collapse. An improvement was effected by placing braces beneath the rafters to prevent them sagging, the braces gradually assuming an arch shape. This however did nothing to prevent the outward thrust until they were lengthened at their lower ends and slotted into corbels, thus taking the thrust lower down and clipping the wall at the same time. Over the chancel of Stockport old church is a fine fourteenth century example of the first type, and at Dennington, Suffolk, of the second, where occasional wall-posts are introduced; in these roofs the rafters are set the same distance apart and are each independent of the other. The addition of the arch-brace also necessitated a hanging post inserted between the ends of the rafters at the apex, into which both they and the braces are mortised, shown in the south aisle roof at Westhall, Suffolk; this type is called an arch-braced roof.

Another method is to place a crossbar or collar two-thirds up between the rafters to strut them apart, with curved braces beneath the collar supporting the rafters at two points and forming a rough kind of arch (104). There are several intermediate types before we come to the collar proper used in the Norfolk churches of Middleton, Southacre, and East Winch. This method is developed in the south-west of England by shaping the struts into semi-circles resting upon the wall-plates. Fine examples at Burrington with open rafters, and decorated panelling at Cullompton (108), both in Devon, and a glorious example at Shepton Mallet in Somerset. Celures were constructed in this form at Lapford and Hennock, Devon. Wall-plates were gradually improved by placing horizontal timbers on either edge of the wall, tenoned together by cross-pieces called sole-plates, the rafter pitching upon the outer edge, with a short post or ashlar-piece flush with the inner wall wedged between the rafter and the inner plate, forming a broad foot for the roof. It was further improved by placing the inner wall timber at a lower level than the outer, allowing the sole-piece to be tenoned directly into the ashlar-piece, preventing the roof from slipping. Both these varieties of roof are called collar and trussed rafter.

There are countless ways of applying decoration to the many types of roofs which, while effectively altering the appearance,

103 LLANGYNHAFEL, DENBIGHSHIRE

104 LLANARMON DENBIGHSHIRE

QUEEN POST ROOF

do not interfere with the construction. The wall-plate is an important line for enrichment, either with trails, bosses or angels, with solid or perforated tracery; at Framlingham, Suffolk (106) and St. Peter Mancroft, Norwich, the wall-plate is designed as a tierceron vault of a screen, each fan springing from an elongated wall-post, the whole completed with a carved bressummer beam forming a purlin to the roof which appears beyond this decorative border.

The hammer-beam roof is a development of the wall-plate noted above. The sole-piece is projected beyond the inner surface of the wall and supported by a wall-post and arch-brace, thus becoming a hammer-beam. On the end of the projecting beam a queen post is erected with an arch-brace supporting the rafters, lessening the span of the roof. This construction prevents the roof slipping, reducing the thrust, placing the strain lower down. In a wide roof this system of bracketing out is further developed by supporting the rafters at additional points and producing the double hammer-beam which is one of the fine accomplishments of the fifteenth century carpenter and carver. The home of the hammer-beam is East Anglia, but it is found elsewhere, especially North Wales, where it is combined with the arch-brace (103), each type alternating; the finest, perhaps at Cilcain, Flintshire, of monastic origin. An early example is at Thornham, Norfolk; there is a fine sequence of richly carved single hammer-beam roofs in Norfolk and Suffolk; of the former Cawston, Necton, Upwell and Wymondham; in Suffolk at Badingham, Earl Stonham (107), and Fressingfield. The north transept at Ely has a splendid roof in which the hammers are formed into angels as they are at Necton, Upwell and West Walton; at Ely a second series terminates the base of the wall-posts. Of double hammer-beam roofs Grundisburgh, Rattlesden, Woolpit and Worlingworth in Suffolk are good examples, the majority designed to harbour three flights of angels; now unfortunately many are missing; in all these roofs the raftering is left exposed. An exceptional specimen at Needham Market is placed over an aisleless nave; the roof is however designed to have aisles which are suspended from a ove, a veritable display of dexterity and craftsmanship.

Ceilings of timber were employed as the late angel roof over the Suffolk chapel at Ewelme, Oxfordshire, or the early flat ceiling on the nave at Waltham Abbey painted with elaborate diamonds and scenes, as is the coffered roof over the nave at Peterborough; another example of similar shape covers the nave of Ely.

THE LAYOUT AND PLAN OF CHURCHES OF VARIOUS TYPES

FROM the commencement of the Middle Ages English church architecture was the practical response to the needs of worship; as ritual was gradually elaborated a suitable building was provided for it in the development of constructional planning. There was however a difference between the development of religious observance and that of building; the first through constant usage and tradition became stabilized, whereas building slowly sloughed off its immaturities and grew self-reliant, scientifically sound and a simplified form of construction. Mediaeval architecture was never a fire sent down from heaven; it was an evolution, inevitable when once begun, and only stayed in a new age by the change of temperament toward religion, with its outlook towards freshly discovered continents, and its revived interest in classical learning and architecture.

For the origins of mediaeval church planning we have to hark back in time to the Romans, their pillared basilicas forming the upper church and the catacombs representing the crypts. Willis and Baldwin Brown state that the earliest cathedral at Canterbury was of basilican form, with an apse at either end and a crypt to the east; Bede tells us that this building was constructed through the labours of the Roman believers. It was repaired and altered by St. Augustine; about 750 St. Cuthbert added the chapel of St. John, and in 940 Bishop Odo both enlarged and heightened the church. Another early plan of Roman origin has been excavated under the destroyed church at Silchester; this plan however approximates more closely to the churches of North Africa than to those of Italy. There were two other sources from which the church plan was evolved, the Celtic square-ended type, and the later apsidal east-end favoured by the Italian missioners. The earlier square-end seen at Escomb was British, whereas the apse was foreign, its general use the result probably of the inability to make a good workmanlike job of a squared corner; for whatever reason, the apse was followed from the days of St. Augustine until the close of the Norman period, when its use became sporadic; from the thirteenth century onwards the square end was dominant, possibly due partly to the influence exercised on architecture by the Cistercian Order.

Saxon churches were planned in several ways, the result of an admixture of races and dogmas, Roman, Celtic, Italian, Gaulish, Danish and Saxon, each contributing a quota. Bradford-on-Avon was planned with lateral chapels or porches, in which an altar was placed, as was the first St. Pancras; primarily however their purpose was for a burial place and they communicated by narrow doorways both externally and internally; they foreshadow the later development of transepts. Wing has an apsidal east-end with a crypt beneath which was also

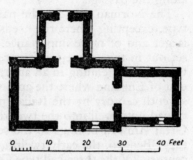

BRADFORD-ON-AVON SAXON CHURCH

the plan at Brixworth. Escomb has the square Celtic east-end; Monkwearmouth a porch tower; other towers are the axial example at Langford, Oxfordshire, and the central one at Breamore, Hampshire. In addition to central there were western axial and independent towers, also towers which formed both the church and a habitation combined, as at Barton-on-Humber. The early basilican plan was not much favoured by the Saxon builders, this form of early Christian continuity however is shown at Brixworth, Wing and the later Great Paxton. For some little time after 1066 the Saxon small church plan was continued, especially in the Lincolnshire districts which were remote from the main stream.

The crypt was important from the beginning, this is seen in the early churches erected by St. Wilfred at Hexham and Ripon; others are found at Lastingham, Wing and Repton. Their purpose was for the burial of distinguished ecclesiastics, who upon their decease rose rapidly to the status of saints. Crypts were planned with both an entrance and an exit within the church,

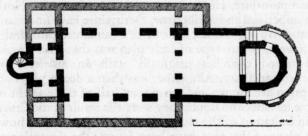

BRIXWORTH NORTHAMPTONSHIRE

not only for the convenience of performing rites within the reliquary, but for the admittance of pilgrims who were allowed to see the relics through an opening in the wall while passing along the passage.

The Norman plan for the parish church was of the aisleless type, excepting where the needs of a town required something larger and of more importance. These aisleless buildings were set out in two, three, or four cells or compartments, the sanctuary usually ending in an apse; this is noticeable in the southeast of England where the apse was first introduced in the early seventh century by the Italian missioners; the type being continued until well into the twelfth century. Of the two-cell type, Great Amwell belongs to the second half of the eleventh century; Bengeo, the early twelfth, and Copford later in the same century. Of the three-cell type Castle Rising is eleventh, Isleham the first quarter and Birkin and Moccas the second quarter of the twelfth century, the last half includes Easton, Kilpeck and Steetley; all these buildings show remains sufficient to be recognizable, and from them we may form an excellent idea of this mode of planning. In this cell type it is seldom we find the outer walls as an unbroken line, for each compartment was planned starting from the west to be a little less in scale than the preceding. Inside, the compartments were divided by arches into nave, choir and sanctuary. There is both beauty and dignity in a series of arches seen in perspective, especially when they are plain and severe such as we find at Peterchurch and Moccas; at Kilpeck however the arches are redundant in decoration. These three examples are all situated in the county of Hereford. Where a four-cell church has existed as at Peterchurch, it indicates an axial tower. Square-ended sanctuaries were built concurrently with the apse; fine examples of this type are to be found at Iffley and Cassington, Oxfordshire, and Stewkley, Buckinghamshire. All these churches retain their axial towers.

Of the parochial plan of a larger church with aisles, Castor, Northamptonshire, Hemel Hempstead, Hertfordshire, Norham, Northumberland and Melbourne, Derbyshire have fine examples of central towers, the last set out as a miniature cathedral with three towers. A rare type of early plan was that with circular or round naved churches originally with an aisleless apsidal chancel or sanctuary. Altogether less than a dozen plans of this description are known and more than half of these are in ruins. In some instances no doubt they were the result of the Crusades, built in imitation of the Holy Sepulchre at Jerusalem; however earlier plans of this type have been found: the eleventh century

108 CULLOMPTON, DEVON

107 EARL STONHAM, SUFFOLK

abbey church of St. Augustine at Canterbury had a nave fifty-four feet in diameter, and the still earlier one at Abingdon Abbey, begun by St. Athelwold about the year 960; a contemporary description telling us that it had a round-ended quire, a circular nave of a span twice the length of the chancel and a round tower, probably placed above the nave. Several of these churches belonged to either the Order of the Hospital of St. John the Baptist founded 1099 or the Order of the Temple founded 1118, which became established in England in 1140 and 1135 respectively; but a few of their churches had round naves and this plan was not persisted in with later buildings.

The religious requirements of the cathedral, monastery and collegiate church were of an entirely different order from that of the parish church both in purpose and size. At first the parish church had a single priest to look after the needs of the parish-ioners; whereas the greater buildings housed large numbers of either regular monks or secular canons, whose home it

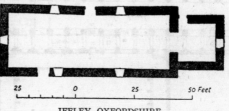

IFFLEY, OXFORDSHIRE

was, and whose duties included the perpetual praise and worship of God. To this end and for this purpose several altars were necessary, with ample room for processions. In the beginning only a few monks in a community were ordained, these looked after the spiritual needs of the brethren; later however as more of the brethren became priests further altars had to be provided for celebrating. The plan for the greater churches had in view the housing of altars considered essential, with accommodation for static worship in addition to processions. In its earliest state this type of church required at least four bays for the quire and presbytery; the ritual quire was often placed forward under the crossing. A processional path round the quire was also desired with additional chapels radiating from it for further altars. The transepts butting against the central tower had both a con-structional as well as a ritual purpose, for they helped to uphold the tower and provided further accommodation for altars. In one or other of the transepts were placed the night stairs from the dormitory down which the brethren came for their night services in the quire. Fencing the quire to the west was the pulpitum, a stone platform at least a bay wide, backing the stalls on its eastern side and providing a space for two altars on either side the central doorway to the west. A bay in front of the pulpitum stood the Rood screen, with a central nave altar placed between two doorways through which the procession passed on the return to the quire. The cloister side of the nave provided two doorways into the eastern and western alleyways for the procession to leave the church and re-enter it after blessing the garth buildings; the great west doorway was only

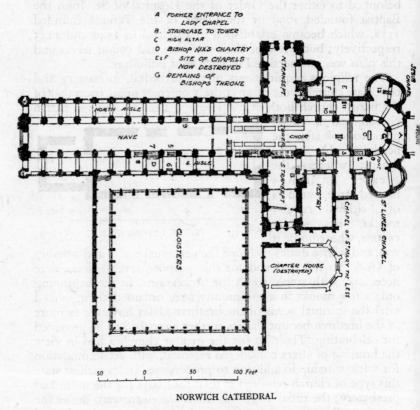

A FORMER ENTRANCE TO
     LADY CHAPEL
B. STAIRCASE TO TOWER
C HIGH ALTAR
D BISHOP NIX'S CHANTRY
E&F SITE OF CHAPELS
     NOW DESTROYED
G REMAINS OF
     BISHOPS THRONE

50   0   50   100 Feet

NORWICH CATHEDRAL

used for the more important festivals. The nave—often of great length—Norwich is of fourteen bays, and St. Albans thirteen—provided for further altars, placed before the piers at St. Albans, so that in several of these churches there were from ten to fifteen altars at the Suppression; in fact Durham had twenty-eight, Salisbury twenty-two, and Exeter at least seventeen.

Early Norman plans are distinguished for the shortness of their eastern arms, their long naves, and the use of the apse for quire, aisles and chapels. Foundations have been excavated of at least twenty-five churches of this character, the eastern ter-

mination showing several methods of treatment; the aisle encircling the quire from which radiated chapels as at Norwich and Gloucester, this last of two storeys. Where the aisles finished in separate apses independent of the central one they were placed either in close proximity, as formerly at St. Albans and Durham (this last circular within and square without), or separated, as at Chertsey. The intriguing plan at Binham shows the quire, aisles and transept chapels forming seven graduating apses, the quire as the largest and furthest extended of the series. Radiating chapels in many examples were semi-circular or horseshoe shaped, and at Norwich with additional semicircular sanctuaries attached. At Leominster the foundations show the chapels as a complete circle. During the various mediaeval rebuildings the majority of apses large and small disappeared; three however remain and give some idea of their original appearance; St. Bartholomew's, Smithfield (78), and the quires at Norwich (82) and Peterborough; the first is a restoration from above the main arcade, the two others have been transformed and enriched by fifteenth century additions to both clerestory and vault; the apsidal chapels at Romsey and Christchurch, Hampshire, are largely unaltered in form as far as the exterior goes.

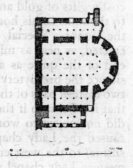

WORCESTER CATHEDRAL
CRYPT

The Normans continued the early practice of erecting their quires upon crypts, but of more spacious size, often sufficient to form underground churches; they are two-aisled at Winchester, three at Gloucester and four at Worcester, and all have groined vaulting with, in several instances, decorated cushion capitals. They are found under quires which possess semi-circular ambulatories and radiating chapels; at Winchester the crypt extends under the eastern chapel, at Canterbury and Gloucester under the radiating chapels. In lesser churches they were placed beneath the chancels as at St. Peter-in-the-East, Oxford (94), and at Berkswell, Warwickshire. These crypts are wholly picturesque, and a vista of the multiplication of piers and arches radiating from different points gives a sense of mystery combined with the strength required to support the immense weight of the structure raised upon them above ground. The shrines of the saints were kept within these crypts, which perhaps accounts for their size for the accommodation of pilgrims.

Both in ritual and building the period between 1140 and 1240 was one of evolution and development. It included the constructional change from the round to the pointed arch and the powerful influence exercised upon planning and construction by the Cistercian Order upon architecture in England. Other important factors in the modification and alteration of the original plans included the growing cults of Mariolatry and relic worship; for the relics of the saints were brought up from the crypts to be given a place of honour behind the high altar, raised upon bases of stone or marble where all could view the costly gifts of gold and jewels which adorned the shrines, given to the saint in his honour and for his intervention on behalf of the donors. Special chapels in honour of the B.V.M. were erected, as near as might be to the high altar, either at the east end of the quire as at Exeter (113) and Chichester, or by the side of the presbytery as at Ely (115), or sometimes forming the two eastern bays of the quire itself as at Worcester and Beverley; that is of course if the saint to whom the church was dedicated did not object to women as did St. Cuthbert of Durham, who caused the Lady chapel to be moved from the east (near his shrine) to the west end beyond his pale. Another instance of a western Lady chapel was at Glastonbury, built upon the earliest chapel founded there.

The constructional change from the round arch to the pointed did not of necessity alter the plan if it altered the construction, but the architecture of the Cistercian Order eventually overcame the stronghold of Benedictine and Cluniac building, eliminating their fortress-like style and decorative redundancies and bringing them into line with a new austerity. The tenets of this second wave of religious revival were plainness and severity; it was owing to the early adherence to these principles that Cistercian architecture came so near to perfection, for it relied entirely upon excellent proportions and delicate mouldings for its effect. At this time, before the alembic which produced the characteristic English style, architecture was like that of the Saxon period of mixed origin, a combination of Normandy, the "Isle de France" and Burgundy; it was the last however which finally predominated. The "Isle de France" influenced the south, the finest example being the quire of Westminster Abbey; it had no abiding place except perhaps in window design. The Yorkshire building of the Cistercian Order sent a second message from the north (the first was that of the Celtic missioners), a message of the austere, constructionally minded, square-ended style to the south of England.

In their first buildings however the Cistercians had the short

quire of the time, as at Kirkstall and Waverley; the naves were often of extraordinary length and at Waverley unaisled. Apart from the fact that the ritual quire was usually placed under the crossing and into the first bay of the nave, the long nave was a necessity, used for the lay brethren who at first formed the second half of a Cistercian community, and who had their own services to fit in with their hours of labour. The need for space can be understood when it is realized that at the close of the twelfth century, Ailred of Rievaulx had 740 men under his care. In the beginning the lay brothers were an added advantage in that they could erect temporary lodgings for the monks at a new site until more permanent housing could be provided. They were the pioneers in agriculture for which the Order became famous and by whose initiative their herds and flocks became the founda-tion of the prosperity of England in the middle ages.

The second half of the twelfth century was par-ticularly interesting, for it displayed many varieties of planning and design when the merging of the Romanesque into the mediaeval style took place,

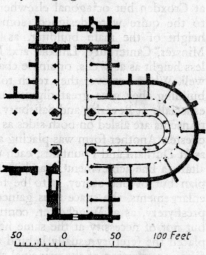

BEAULIEU ABBEY CHEVET

each building having some particular treatment in its approach. The quires and presbyteries first erected became quickly inadequate for the increasing ritual, and rebuilding often began at the east end before the church had been completed at the west. It was quite feasible to rebuild and enlarge the short eastern arms, when it was a practical impossibility to reconstruct a ponderous and massive Romanesque nave; for it took over two centuries to remove and replace King Edward's nave at Westminster, and it was still incomplete at the Suppression; one reason why so many Norman naves are still in existence at the present day. In this general rebuilding of quires the form of apse largely disappeared, giving place to the square end, and although later one or two examples of the French chevet were designed and built, as at Beaulieu, they were quite exceptional.

In the enlargements of quire and presbytery, plans show much diversity; there was the square end across which a processional path with chapels was placed, running beyond the main structure as in the Cistercian examples at Abbey Dore, Byland and Waverley. It is probable that Vale Royal had the same though at a later date, for there is a record of twelve chapels being erected at the east end. In the first rebuilding at York the existing crypt suggests a square ended processional path similar to Jervaulx and Romsey carried out within the main structure. At Croxden, Hailes, Tewkesbury and Westminster however, the apse was retained with their radiating chapels, circular in form at Croxden but octagonal elsewhere. Lesser transepts attached to the quire were designed, sometimes reaching to the full height of the main building, as at Salisbury (35), Beverley Minster, Canterbury, Lincoln and later at York; sometimes of less height as at Wells, or single chapels as at Exeter and Southwell. When however they reach to the full height of the main building they give great dignity and richness to the exterior, especially at Beverley and Salisbury. In a few examples the main transepts are aisled on both sides as at Beaulieu, Wells and Winchester. Another form was placing a transept across the east end, as at Durham and Fountains, each called the chapel of the nine altars, a fine achievment in architectural vistas. A rather similar plan but of one storey is to be found at Hereford. In these enlargements, the space thus gained was given to an extended presbytery, as at Winchester, continuing behind the high altar but not of necessity at the same height. Within this space was placed the feretory usually behind the reredos screen and used for the protection of the principal shrine, the surrounding walls often lined with cupboards also containing lesser relics; in the near vicinity was a raised watching chamber for the custodian, which may still be seen at St. Albans and Oxford, both chambers constructed of timber.

It was during the seond half of the twelfth century that the Lady chapel became an essential part of church design. The Galilee at Durham (7) and the chapel of St. Mary at Glastonbury are dated 1175 and 1186 respectively. It is curious that in both instances these early chapels are placed at the west end of important churches. There are no Lady chapels in the Cistercian lay out, for the dedication of all their churches to the B.V.M. made an additional chapel for that purpose unnecessary. In the majority of cases the Lady chapel is placed east beyond the presbytery; many have been destroyed but excellent examples remain, Chester of the thirteenth century (much restored), Exeter (113), Lichfield (83, 121) and Wells of the fourteenth century, and of later date at Gloucester and Winchester. When this position was found inconvenient, a place was chosen in near proximity to the quire, as at Ely (115, 116), and in the first erections at Bristol, Tewkesbury and Wells; these three were however later superseded by chapels at the east end of the church. Another form was to combine the Lady chapel with the main structure, using the last two eastern bays for this purpose; this type is found at Beverley and Worcester of the thirteenth century, Selby of the fourteenth and in the last

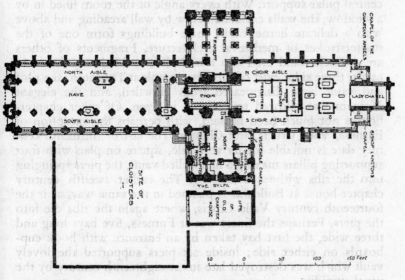

WINCHESTER CATHEDRAL

phase at Bristol and York. In many ways this form adds to the nobility of the church, extending the ridge of the main building and lengthening the quire; inside however it is not so successful for it lacks unity and cohesion as well as intimacy and seclusion. In design and detail several of these special chapels are both handsome and lovely, the wonderfully enriched example at Ely (116), the graceful structure at Lichfield (83, 121), and the fifteenth century chapel at Gloucester with its exquisite vaulting and additional chapels are specimens. Others we have lost include Norwich and Tewkesbury. Mention should be made of the twelfth century Becket's crown at Canterbury and the sixteenth century chapel of Henry VII at Westminster (126). This magnificent structure although dedicated to the B.V.M. was and still is in glorification of Henry VII and is still called by his name; it is the richest and most resplendent structure of its kind in England.

Chapter-houses are a study by themselves; in shape, square, oblong, octagonal, circular and polygonal, those designed in the last mentioned form are the loveliest, erected with or without a central pillar. Many have been destroyed, but a number remain for our appreciation and enjoyment. The polygonal type date from between 1200 and 1300 and include Lincoln about 1200, Westminster 1250, Salisbury 1260, Wells (50) 1260 to 1290, Southwell 1280 (60), (114), and York 1290 to 1300, these last two examples built by the Yorkshire masons with no central pillar support. With every angle of the room filled in by a window, the walls enriched below by wall arcading and above with a delicate lierne vault, these buildings form one of the masterstrokes of mediaeval architecture. Fragments of others are at Cockersand used as a burial place and half smothered in earth; three sides exist of a lovely example at Thornton; the roof and vault have disappeared from Howden, and the elegant Margam was allowed to collapse in 1799. Of other chapter-houses not much need be said, with perhaps the exception of Furness, Valle Crucis, and Chester. The last of thirteenth century date is notable for its vestibule, square on plan with four supporting pillars making a nine-celled vault, the piers springing into the ribs without a capping. The earlier twelfth century chapter-house at Buildwas is planned in the same way, as is the fourteenth century Valle Crucis, where again the ribs die into the piers. Perhaps the finest was at Furness, five bays long and three wide, the first bay taken by an entrance with book cupboards on either side; inside six piers supported the lovely vault which was destroyed late in the eighteenth century by the usual stupidity.

Cloisters were attached to secular cathedrals as well as monastic and collegiate establishments. The first designs were brought over from France and were quite unsuitable for our bleak climate. The inner walls were part of the conventual buildings, the walls facing the garth composed of sets of elegant twin piers set edgewise, placed upon a low stone wall, the alleyways boarded above with a sloping roof; in this design there was no protection from the elements although it was the centre of monastic activities (118). By the thirteenth century however the cloisters were windowed and later glazed, with the addition of a stone vaulted roof; and those remaining at Salisbury (117), Gloucester and Lacock are a joy to behold, every detail carefully thought out and aptly fitted to the needs and requirements.

The parish church however took a different line in that its development was usually haphazard and accorded with the local needs, generally piecemeal in character, which perhaps gives to an unrestored church its chief charm and interest to the student. After the twelfth century the churches grew a little bit here and a little bit there, an aisle was added, or the chancel lengthened, a tower was built or a porch, and later a chantry chapel or two were fitted into the scheme. What one church was doing in the way of enlargement had little bearing upon the next for it was a matter of needs, or piety, or both. In the fourteenth century there was much rebuilding and replanning with wider aisles, and again towards the close of the fifteenth century when many churches were remodelled to meet new ideas and furnishings.

A common method of enlarging the nave by the addition of an aisle, was first to build its outer walls to the roof line, leaving an opening through which waste could be removed. When the walls were completed, an arcade was broken through the original wall; first the wall was cut away where the piers were to stand, leaving the rest of the walling as a support while the arches were

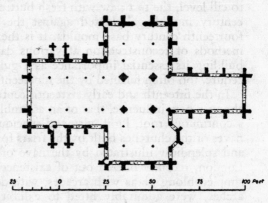

PATRINGTON, YORKSHIRE

constructed, then all surplus stone was removed through the gap, which was finally closed. It is therefore not unusual to find the remains of early windows, even of Saxon origin above, say, a fourteenth century arcade. Again as each aisle was probably erected at a different date and both built from the outside it is not surprising to find that the arcades do not match each other across the nave. Not that churches were not at times built or rebuilt at a single period, reflecting the style of the time in its completeness. Darlington (29) and West Walton are of the early thirteenth century; Heckington, Hawton and Patrington of the fourteenth century; but the average parish church as it was before restoration was an assemblage of styles which sometimes blend in a wonderful way, and others do not. As John Bilson wrote concerning Beverley St. Mary:

"Its original plan has been entirely transformed by a succession of changes and alterations, and we cannot understand, far less are we justified in criticizing, what has come down to us, unless we have succeeded in realizing to what extent the builders of each section of the work were controlled and limited by what already existed, to which their new work had to be connected. . . . It is idle to criticize such a church as if it were of one design, instead of what it is, the result of at least a dozen different building campaigns; and it is no small tribute to the skill of the builders of that latest time . . . the period which some writers have been so fond of stigmatizing as 'debased' . . . that they succeeded so admirably in giving an air of dignity and unity to a conglomeration of works of so many different periods."

Even when the original walls were left standing new windows were inserted, or as at Malpas, Cheshire, the original was left to cill level, the rest new with fresh buttressing having fifteenth century mouldings planted against the earlier wall with its fourteenth century base moulds. It is the following out of the methods of reconstruction at various dates which gives to a building its essential importance as a guide to mediaeval procedure, too often falsified by the nineteenth century restorer.

In the fifteenth and early sixteenth centuries church planning shows a new influence, that of an assembly hall enclosed under a continuous roof, light, airy and spacious; a reflection of the naves of the churches built by the friars for preaching purposes, and splendidly illustrated by the nave of the Austin Friars in London, recently blitzed out of existence by the Huns. These simple oblong plans with arcades, with delicate piers and wide arches, were admirably fitted to exhibit the treasures of the church in glass, wood, and stone, separated by vaulted and galleried screens, a reversion to the early western undivided church, but glorified and enhanced by fifteenth century craftsmanship. The grim and rough fortress type of towers in Pembrokeshire and Glamorganshire has already been mentioned, and the planning of the village churches of Wales may here be discussed. The majority of mediaeval churches in the Principality, especially in the north, must always architecturally speaking have been a law unto themselves, a little primitive in effort and local in construction. The average church was a single cell divided by a loft and screen. These small buildings devoid of arcades and chancel arches were entirely outside English influence, indeed remote from any trend except their own. The people had insufficient means to employ travelling masons, as was customary in England, masons who had gained their knowledge and experience in monastic and cathedral yards.

These small churches, whether built in the folds of the mountains, upon the bare uplands, or by the shore, were usually

116 DETAIL OF INSIDE ARCADING

115 ELY, LADY CHAPEL, EAST END,
FOURTEENTH CENTURY

117 SALISBURY, LATE THIRTEENTH CENTURY

118 NEWMINSTER, NORTHUMBERLAND, EARLY THIRTEENTH CENTURY

constructed with local materials and by local labour, homely and sufficient for the communities they served. On account of these things they are of exceptional interest, but through the neglect into which they were allowed to fall in the eighteenth century, they have required considerable reclamation in addition to that century's clumsy insertions of windows and doorways, plastering under roofs and enlarging Georgian pewing until they actually cluttered up the sanctuary. Unfortunately the result of reclamation has tended to become wholesale rebuilding on English lines, and many churches were deserted or demolished for more convenient if incongruous buildings within the villages. The architects employed did not consider it a part of their responsibility to preserve the local types; they had not been instructed when they were apprentices that there ever were such things; all they knew was "Victorian gothic", which was good enough for them, and was the Open Sesame to church work.

To the original builders it was of small consequence whether their windows were square or pointed, mullioned or traceried, so long as the structure was weather-proof. Indeed windows were apt to let in the weather, and often the sides towards the sea-borne tempests were constructed without either windows or doorways; likewise the churches were kept low to withstand the gales and snow. The thick walls were often put together with boulders, and when completed were lime-washed for protection; as the early masons treated their stonework in England, for lime-wash is a wonderful preservative. What is more charming than a white-washed church set amidst dark yews, against a hillside of greenery or russet, perhaps topped by blue sky? These village churches were distinguished from the surrounding farms and houses by having a bell-cot placed upon the west gable and a little cross upon the east, with here and there an occasional stone porch.

When enlargements were required their methods were simple; it was easier to tack on a chapel or transept to the chancel than to endeavour to construct a stone arcade for an aisle; it had another advantage in enabling the congregation to be nearer the centre of worship. Welsh naves were narrow and the walls thick to withstand the outward thrust of their favourite form of roof construction, an arch-brace without wall-posts. The reasons for the absence of chancel arch and arcade were as much a question of capacity as of tradition, and in restoration this should be remembered and followed. Nevertheless in building their chapels, the join to the main building had to be faced, and it was usually awkwardly met and without a stone arch.

o

The occupation of the English produced a number of English buildings in Wales, but although the conquerors built many fine churches, their influence was nil apart from monastic structures; the natives did not copy, indeed they would not deign to do so; therefore such churches as Gresford, Mold, Bangor and Clynnog Fawr remained just isolated examples of the English mode in a foreign land, as did the castles and fortified towns.

During the second half of our period, one of the most congenial forms of religious activity was that of prayers for the dead; this entailed the employment of additional priests to serve at the altars which were erected in special enclosures for this purpose. These enclosures or chapels were surprisingly varied in content as well as in position; they attained on occasion to the size of a great chapel, such as that of Archbishop Zouch at York, 1352, or they could be so tiny as to leave bare room for the ministrant, as in a canopied tomb at Edington. Chapels were erected in stone or were fenced by screens from their immediate surroundings; they were placed in the nave, chancel, quire or aisles or for them special buildings were made both within and without the main fabric of the church; indeed there seems to have been no place or position excluded to them with the exception of the high altar which was the cynosure and the magnet forming the central attraction, for the nearer to the high altar the more sacred and important the position for burial. These chantry chapels by their multiplicity of form and design were a prominent and remarkable addition to the enrichment and adornment not only of the average parish church but of the abbey and cathedral; in many cases indeed their retention has, although now shorn of their furnishings, remained one of the more interesting and valuable sources of information regarding the memorials of the past.

A complete description of their varied form would entail a consideration both of the architecture and craftsmanship for at least two hundred years. They however do not enter into this section excepting where they form an addition to the building, such as the delightful examples at Potterne and Devizes in Wiltshire, both by the same master builder, and the pleasant Egerton chapel at Bunbury in Cheshire. In the greater churches a place could usually be found for them within the buildings, as at Tewkesbury, Ely, Gloucester, Wells and Exeter; it was however otherwise in a small parish church and often a special chapel was added for this purpose, as the Lane aisle, 1526, at Cullompton, Devon, or the Dorset aisle, 1502–30, at Ottery St. Mary, both receiving a fine fan vaulted roof. Little chapels were clustered round Lady chapels as at Gloucester and Hereford or near an important entrance as at Lincoln, but architecturally these small additions did little to influence the general plan. Curious positions were sometimes chosen to insure proximity to the high altar; at Westminster Abbey the chantry of Henry V is poised above the ambulatory, literally in mid-air between the high altar and the former Lady chapel. In the destroyed quire at Bridlington Priory the feretory of St. John of Bridlington was elevated; to quote the destroyers of the Priory:

"The Reredose at the highe Alter representyng Criste at the Assumpcyon of our Lady and the xij Appostells, wt dyvers othe great Imagys, beyng of a great heyght, ys excellently well wrought and as well gylted, and betwene the same and the Est Wyndow ys Saynt John of Brydlyngton Shryne, in a fayre Chappel on hyhe, having on ayther syde a stayre of Stone for to goo and cume by. Ubdernethe the sayde Shryne be fyve Chappells wt fyve alters and small Tables of Alleblaster and Imag's."

At a late date a chamber was also built over the high vault of the presbytery at Tynemouth Priory.

Many of the lesser churches possessed treasuries for the protection of their valuables; if erected as an addition to the chancel on the north side there was no outside doorway, as at Bunbury and Nantwich in Cheshire; should it take the form of a crypt beneath the high altar, which was convenient when the ground sloped to the east, it was again approached from the inside as at Malpas, Cheshire, and Gresford, Denbighshire, and several other examples might be cited.

were important entrances as at Lincoln; but architecturally these small additions did little to influence the general plan. Various positions were
to the high altar, as at Westminster Abbey, the chantry of Henry V
high altar and the tomb of Lady chapel. In the destroyed chantry at
Bridlington Priory the shrine of St. John of Bridlington was
elevated, to quote the death of the
A are data chambers, also built over the high

SECTION VIII

THE ORGANISATION OF MEDIAEVAL BUILDING

THE CRAFTSMEN

THE question of craftsmen, materials and transport were closely allied to the planning and development of mediaeval building. Unfortunately it is sparsely documented, and on its creative side offers a complete blackout. Fabric rolls relating to building under the aegis of Royalty however are more numerous, and occasionally a few relating to other buildings have been preserved, including Durham, Ely, Exeter and Winchester. From these it is possible to gather information on many points of interest.

During the earlier part of the mediaeval period the position of the mason differed in many particulars from that of other craftsmen in that his work was of a special nature. Dwelling-houses were constructed of timber, masonry being reserved for more important undertakings, castles, cathedrals, churches, monasteries, the king's works and sometimes bridges and gild-halls; but stone was seldom used for more ordinary purposes. Small building jobs were the exception, and many of the greater building schemes took place far away from a town and were more or less self contained. Owing to these circumstances the majority of masons were a scattered community, living in the country upon farm holdings which their families worked, and to which the masons returned for the winter or when work was scarce. This habit seems to have been responsible for the absence of control either by gilds or enactments until a much later date, for their wages were not regulated as in other communities and they made individual bargains; neither were the divisions in labour so strictly enforced, for as occasion demanded, a free-mason would work at a quarry as well as in a lodge where the actual building took place.

The fabric rolls for the first three years of construction of the Royal work at Vale Royal, Cheshire, show that between 1278 and 1280 as many as 131 masons were employed who came from many different parts of England, only seven men came from towns and few had local names; the majority travelled from places where building was in progress as Buildwas, Eynsham, Furness, Leominster, Pershore, Roche, St. Albans and Winchcombe. Their stay at Vale Royal was not prolonged,

119 HEREFORD CATHEDRAL, THE STANBURY CHAPEL

A CHURCH IN THE DERBYSHIRE UPLANDS

usually of a few months' duration when they moved on, in some cases probably working in the erection of the fine fourteenth century churches then rising in Cheshire. Circumstances therefore precluded masons from settling down in a town with a small stone yard of their own; it compelled them to lead a rather nomadic existence, travelling in groups with their own horses and carts, both for safety and company. They do not seem to have been compelled to stay at any one job, excepting in cases where they were impressed by the king for his own work, or that of some great overlord such as the Archbishop of Canterbury who in 1396 received the Royal assent for that purpose. When impressment occurred, the sheriffs of the various counties were instructed to provide their quota of masons for the required work, and any mason refusing was liable to imprisonment. Sometimes impressment so worked out that the king held the majority of skilled masons for his own purposes, all other undertakings suffering in consequence.

In all large building schemes, lodges accommodating from ten to twenty men were provided for the masons in which to work; these were usually single-storeyed timber sheds thatched with straw. At Vale Royal in the roll for 1279 occurs the following entries:

"Paid to Nicholas de Buddewerre with his fellows for making 1400 boards for the new masons workshop 28/- at 2/- a hundred. On Sunday April 7. paid Nicholas the boarder with his fellows for making a 1000 boards for the new masons workshop and for others 20/- at 2/- a hundred. Paid him and his fellows and servants for making 2000 boards for covering the masons workshop and other houses 40/-.

In the fifteenth century both York and Westminster provided each two lodges; these were never intended as hostels but as workshops, and in them the tools of the masons were kept under a supervisor; they were certainly used for the noon siesta and at mealtimes. Hostels were sometimes provided, for at Eton in 1448 the college found fuel and the services of a cook for this purpose. In districts remote from civilization, such as the Cistercian Order chose for their convents, houses had to be provided for the workmen. At Vale Royal in 1278 the carpenters were busy making huts and dwelling-houses for the masons and other workmen and smithies for the smiths both at the quarry and on the site. The plasterers were also employed in making and plastering the houses and workshops and other dwelling-places in the site of the abbey.

Masons were engaged by the week, the month or the year;

occasionally and with certain safeguards for five years or may be for life. At Hereford in 1359 John of Evesham was so engaged; the terms set down were that he was to live in Hereford, work diligently on the fabric, not to work elsewhere, and to teach others placed under his charge; in return he was to have a house at 10/- a year, a white loaf daily and 3/- a week for life. Should illness prevent him from working for one or two weeks his wages stood, if however the time was extended he was only to receive 12 pence a week.

There were many grades of workers in stone, from the master mason to the digger, including both free and rough masons, imagers, carvers, setters and wallers, paviors, tilers, quarriers, scapplers, hewers and diggers. The freemason worked in the finer freestones completing the stone already roughed out by the scappler; he was responsible for cutting the tracery, setting out the vaulting ribs and often carving the details; he sometimes combined this with the actual erection, for this required the utmost skill and precision. The rough masons were usually also setters and wallers, men who built ashlar-faced masonry as well as ordinary rubble walling. Paviors laid the floors, and tilers were the brick layers. At the quarry end were the diggers and hewers of stone, as well as the quarry men and the scapplers; these last consisted in working the stone with a hammer to a given shape, leaving it to be completed by the freemason. Should the quarry be far away from the building site, masons and rough masons had a lodge at the quarry to save the weight and costs of transport.

Tools were usually provided for the masons, or if they brought their own it was the custom that they should be bought, and re-purchased when they left; the tools were kept at the lodge. The following tools occur in the fabric roll for the first year at Vale Royal, together with several unidentified: 64 hatchets at 4½d. each; 4 picks for the quarry 18d.; 2 large hammers for breaking stones 4/-; 36 wedges or chisels 2½d. each; 48 irons for carving stones; 4 sieves for making mortar and 3 buckets for the use of the builders of the walls. Other tools included gavels, trowels, mallets, tracing boards, compasses, squares and plumblines. Tools for rougher work included hoes, shovels, hods and wheel-barrows.

Masons are often accredited with servants, but in what capacity is difficult to state; both masons and wallers required assistants but who provided them is not always shown. Lads were apprenticed to both free and rough masons, serving from seven to ten years. At Vale Royal they are termed diggers and other common workmen; they were employed:

121   EAST END OF LADY CHAPEL, LICHFIELD CATHEDRAL

122 CANTERBURY CATHEDRAL, NAVE, LOOKING NORTH-EAST

"working and levelling a place on which the ground plan of the monastery was to be traced and all the work called the floor space to be cleared filled out, in and levelled. The 'bairdores' working with hand barrows taking large stones to be carved at the masons workshop and outside . . . working with hoes and other tools suitable for digging and making turves and ditches, upon the forming of a pond, from which a water course should flow down to the site of the monastery for making the mortar. . . . Paid William the Fox he being the 44th who were then digging and laying foundations of the church; some are 'bairdores' to the masons workshop, others making ditches and foundations, others making mortar, some carrying this, some throwing the sand, some wheeling barrows, some working at different places in the site of the monastery and each receiving 9d a week."

Certain masons received a cloak and gloves in part payment or as a sign of approval; masons, carpenters and scaffolders were often provided with gauntletted gloves to protect their hands from cuts and splinters.

Wages were paid in advance and varied according to the season of the year. Winter hours were fewer than those of summer and masons' work was often closed down during the winter. At Vale Royal the roll says: each year about November William the Daubour and his men were paid piece rate for plastering the walls and foundations of the church for the winter. Straw was bought, for they paid William of Eyton for 60 thraves of straw for making plaster, and for covering the stonework during the winter.

Although the master mason was on a different footing from the other masons he is usually classed with them in the fabric rolls. At Vale Royal Walter of Hereford received 2/- a day including Sundays, whether he was at Vale Royal or on other business of the king; John of Batile was the under master and received three shillings a week as his understudy. It is probable that Walter rose from a working mason by sheer ability, being a cutter of tracery, but he must have shown unmistakable genius at his job to fill such an important post, for it was important; he was responsible for the building and engaged or dismissed all grades of craftsmen under him, judging them by their capacity for the work for which they were employed. In several instances the master mason was joined with the clerk of works in the disbursement of the fabric monies. After the ecclesiatics had explained their requirements, it lay with the master mason to make the layout and design the building, keeping in close touch with its progress. The king's master masons were often required to be responsible for more than one undertaking; Walter had Vale Royal and Caernarvon Castle; Henry Yevele,

1356, both Westminster Abbey and the Hall. These mediaeval master masons were severely practical men who could use their hands in addition to their heads, and who thoroughly understood their job by practice not from theory or from book learning. Professor Jacks says, "an educated man is one who can do things in which he has never passed an examination," and these men are fine examples of it.

At Exeter 1329 to 1379 the master mason was provided with a house close at hand and although he paid a rent it was kept in repair from the fabric fund. At Worcester in 1316 William of Shockerwick, master mason, was granted a corrody for which he paid sixty pounds; this included a chamber and stable which he was to have for life, every day a monks loaf and a white loaf with two gallons of the best beer; on every flesh day a dish from a joint with two dishes of pottage, and for supper enough for two monks; on fish days what is served to a monk in the refectory.

The early methods of nomenclature are helpful in locating the birthplaces of several mediaeval master masons. William of Wynford, of Winchester, William Shockerwick of Worcester and Henry Yevele of Westminster have all Somerset names, born no doubt within sound of quarries. In each case they must have shown aptitude in their work, for they all occupied positions of grave responsibility. They travelled widely and are found controlling works far from their native homes. Instances are recorded where a master mason for a higher wage transferred his services from one building to another, as William Hyndles from Norwich to York; or when in 1407 the king sent his master mason William of Colchester from Westminster to York. In how far each master had an individual style we do not know, but they were certainly knowledgeable in the latest developments of architecture. Ecclesiastical communities sometimes lent their craftsmen to each other; at Exeter in 1312 Master Thomas of Winchester came over to select the timber for the new bishop's throne and possibly designed it. In 1310 Master John of Glastonbury came to Exeter and removed the stalls from the old quire to the new one, and about the same time Master William of Shockerwick, who was then at Salisbury, was paid a fee for visiting the new work and giving his advice.

The clerk of the works was the man responsible for the fabric fund, not only the expenditure but its collection. At St. Albans the master mason, Hugh of Godelif, was allowed to be so extravagant that the new west front had to be abandoned half-way through. In a convent the sacrist was usually appointed, in other churches a canon, sometimes two, took the office. It is very doubtful if in any case they had anything to do with the actual designing of the fabric, that is apart from suggestions. Mediaeval writers always give the full praise for the work to the head of the church, abbot or bishop or possibly to the sacrist, but never to the master mason. This applies to Alan of Walsingham at Ely whose master mason was John atte Grene; William of Wykeham of Winchester whose master mason was William of Wynford, and Elias of Dereham who is supposed to have designed Salisbury Cathedral. In each case a clerk would be chosen who had both financial ability combined with a taste for architecture, such as Jocelin of Brakelond of Bury St. Edmunds records of Sampson sub-sacrist, "he being master of the workmen did his best that no breach, chink, crack or flaw should be left unrepaired so far as he was able. He also made a great draught of stone and sand for building the great tower of the church. A.D. 1180."

Whilst the foregoing gives to us some knowledge of the type of men who erected these interesting buildings, it gives little clue as to how they were designed or in what manner the development of the style took place. Did it come here a little and there a little or was it an orderly progression of ideas? From the thirteenth century onwards a distinctive treatment of buildings is noticeable in different areas; leaving out the south, which was always more or less under foreign influence, we find that in the west there is a freedom of detail in the thirteenth century not to be found elsewhere. In the fourteenth the northeast showed a style both rich and vital; by the middle of that century the Severn Valley masons had developed a new architectural approach to building, but we are still in the dark as to who originated the arcades at Llandaff, the quire at Guisborough and that of St. Augustine at Bristol, all of them distinct landmarks in mediaeval architecture.

The carpenter was only second in importance to the mason. He was responsible for the scaffolding, making the templets, constructing the roofs and furnishing the church. The king employed a master carpenter as he did a master mason. In the thirteenth century Master Alexander was engaged upon the belfry at Westminster which had a leaded spire of considerable height. Twenty-four carpenters, with nine plumbers, were engaged upon it; it was completed in 1253, William the plumber being master of the leadwork. At Exeter Robert Galmeton was master carpenter when the bishop's throne was erected in 1316, with the carving by William of Membury, both Devonshire men. The king's carpenter from Westminster, William Hurle, was borrowed by Alan of Walsingham during the erection of the great lantern at Ely, receiving a retaining fee of eight pounds during its erection. A little later another king's carpenter, Master Hugh Herland, was about 1398 responsible for the magnificent achievement of constructing the roof over Westminster Hall. More ordinary work however was the lot of the average carpenter, as at Exeter in 1373 when they were employed in the erection of much scaffolding, and for which six pairs of gauntletted gloves were bought for the carpenters to protect their hands while raising the timbers.

A smithy was an essential adjunct to any large undertaking, for the masons and quarriers' tools required constant sharpening as well as making fresh tools; for in mediaeval times tools were made as required generally on the spot. It took seven smiths to forty masons and fifteen quarrymen. At Vale Royal there were smithies both at the quarry and on the site of the monastery. In the earliest accounts are items paid to Bate Malbole of Middlewich for two bellows for the smithy 7/8; for one anvil 2/-; for two hammers 10d.; and for three pincers 12d. To each smith was attached a number of servants who are graded in the wagebook as follows:

"Adam of Neiston, smith 2/- a week; William of Buddeworthe his servant 1/- a week; William of Santa Cruce, collier (charcoal burner) 1/- a week; Rodger of Castro 'portehache' carrying the irons and hatchets of the masons and other tools back to the smithy to be repaired 8d a week; William of Torperlegh servant for the bellows and striker 10d a week and finally John Kyde his boy 7d a week."

Iron was purchased from William and Robert of Newcastle (Staffordshire?) 60 dozen of iron at 12d. a dozen; each dozen containing six pieces, also 15 dozen from Bate Malbone at 10d. the same year. A little steel was bought and large quantities of nails of various sorts. During the first year they amounted to 31,000.

MATERIALS

The majority of the varied stones found in England were worked and used by the masons for building purposes, from the easy freestones to the intractable Kentish rag and Cornish granite. Stone found in the immediate neighbourhood of the site was used whenever feasible; when however the district was devoid of good building stone it was either imported, as from Caen along the south coast, or other materials were brought into service. In Essex, brick and timber were substituted, in East Anglia flints bedded in mortar. Building stones are divided into oolites, limestones, chalks, gritstones, sandstones, and marbles;

123 WINCHESTER CATHEDRAL, NAVE, FROM NORTH AISLE

124   CHAPEL OF ST. GEORGE, WINDSOR, LOOKING EAST

all these classes of stone were quarried during the whole period, their differing characteristics influencing both design and construction. Quarries were owned or leased as circumstances dictated. Barnack, Northamptonshire, was one of the well known quarries, the property of the convent of Peterborough providing a valuable addition to the funds of the monastery. Barnack supplied the stone not only for Peterborough, but for Ely, Crowland, Thorney, Ramsey and Norwich. It was practically worked out before the close of the mediaeval period. Doulting in Somerset owned by Glastonbury Abbey was its main source of supply and it was also used by Wells; the stone of these two quarries was a coarse oolite, but fine oolites came from Dundry near Bristol, and Ancaster in Lincolnshire, which later supplied the grey stone used in Lincoln Cathedral. Other freestones were at Headington and Taynton in Oxfordshire; Ketton, Rutland, supplied Bury St. Edmunds, and Brinstead, Isle of Wight, was the source for Quarre Abbey and the exterior walls at Beaulieu.

Mediaeval quarrying had not the present-day facilities for pumping, haulage, mechanical cranes and gunpowder; it was indeed a heavy and toilsome job. The quarries could not be excavated deeply owing to flooding and the only remedy was the use of buckets. The side of a hill or an escarpment of rock was chosen and an outcrop of rock was also useful. The average mediaeval quarry was small, about twenty-five feet across, though of course Barnack was much greater. This accounts for the practice of individual quarrying still carried on at Purbeck. In the Vale Royal accounts payments at the quarry of sandstone at Edisbury hill included such entries as:

"paid to Robert of Inis, Paul of Alueton, John Cradoc and Richard Louekin, masters, each working in his quarry by himself with his servants and each receiving 18d a week. Paid to Richard the Grant, master of a quarry by himself, receiving 18d a week."

Ordinary quarriers were paid at the rate of 10d. a week but the quarriers and cutters with heavy mallets were paid 12d. a week.

Magnesian limestones were quarried in Yorkshire at Huddlestone and at Theresdale. This valuable area was divided up between various religious communities, York, Drax, Howden and Thornton and later Eton College, who either owned the quarries or as at York in 1386 leased one for eighty years. Selby also bought three acres for a quarry from the Prior of Marton. A shelly limestone called Chilmark was used in the erection of Salisbury Cathedral, a chalky limestone at Beer in Devon was owned by the chapter at Exeter. The Ham Hill stone in Somerset of a lovely orange tone was used at Sherborne

Abbey. Other limestones are found at Portland and Bath. Grit-stones are in Lancashire, Yorkshire, Derbyshire, Durham and Northumberland. The Abbey of Kirkstall near Leeds is con-structed of a local millstone grit called Framley Hall, coarse-grained, extremely hard and lasting, but precluding fine detail. The walls are fine axed, diagonally for plain walling and verti-cally and horizontally for the mouldings. Durham owned their own quarries which were in the vicinity of the building site, particular stone for decoration was brought by water.

Sandstones lie through Cumberland, Lancashire, Cheshire, Staffordshire, Salop, Herefordshire and also at Reigate. Chester Castle and Abbey were built from stone quarried just outside the northgate of the city. Vale Royal had quarries at Edisbury six miles away and other old Cheshire quarries are at Storeton Wirral, and at Runcorn. For interior work and enrichment several marbles were available. Purbeck from the Isle of Corfe was the most important. It was used largely during the first two hundred years for piers, shafting, pavements, effigies and tombs. Frosterley or Stanhope marble from Weardale, Durham, was used in the north in place of Purbeck. Petworth, Sussex, was more confined in its area of use. Other stones used for decoration and delicate carving included Clunch, a type of chalk, and alabaster from Chellaston in Derbyshire. The former was used for the wonderful carved arcade round the Lady-chapel at Ely, the latter for tombs, effigies, and panels. Both materials when first quarried are rather easy to work, hardening upon exposure to the air similar to Caen stone.

In the early periods of quarrying, blocks of stone were scappled as far as possible to a uniform size, about the weight a man could carry on his shoulder; later however as working conditions and masoncraft improved this became unnecessary, and the quarrymen in splitting up the beds of rock, cut stones of varying size without having to consider their uniformity. The wallers seem to have bedded the ashlar as it came straight from the quarry without taking any special care to lay it in level courses. This method or the lack of it has fortunately resulted in giving a varied and diverse face to the walls, weather-ing to a richness of tone even on the plainest surfaces. In many restorations this quality has been ignored, especially in France, with the result that a wall restored in the modern monotonous manner is as far from mediaeval tradition and usage as the modern imitation of Norman crudities chiselled to a fine edge; a juxtaposition of absurdities, surely another lesson to the mechanically minded who would reduce everything to a dead level of a common denominator.

125 KING'S COLLEGE CHAPEL, CAMBRIDGE, LOOKING EAST

126 CHAPEL OF THE B.V.M., KNOWN AS HENRY VII'S
CHAPEL, AT WESTMINSTER ABBEY

The greater mediaeval churches were usually covered with lead or copper, as were the majority of parish churches in the late fifteenth and early sixteenth centuries; otherwise stone tiles or brick tiles were in use. The quarries at Stonesfield, twelve miles from Oxford, supplied much of the roofing material for that county, small graded yellowish stones forming a charming covering to either a stone house or church. In Cheshire, stone slabs from Kerridge near Bollington were extensively used, especially for timbered churches and houses.

Colour plays an important part in the impression a building conveys to the spectator; the rich red sandstone of Chester when first seen obscures by its glow the rather unattractive exterior of the cathedral. The pale rose of Melrose, the pearly quality of the magnesian limestone at York, Selby and Howden, and the yellow of the ironstone at Lincoln, all give an individuality and charm to the various buildings. Within, the luminous orange of the Ham Hill stone at Sherborne, and the grey green of the unpolished Purbeck of the nave piers at Exeter (96) are the things which linger in the memory of these places. The green of the Reigate stone and that of the Forest of Dean, the purple of the ironstone used at Crediton, Devon, and in many a church in Northamptonshire, in addition to the bluish-grey and plum colour of the granite at St. David's are inescapable impressions when the actual constructional details have largely faded from the mind through time, leaving only a sense of colour and beauty.

TRANSPORT

In the erection of a building the cost in transport of material often outweighed that of labour and materials together, especially if stone had to be conveyed long distances from quarry to site; the methods employed therefore needed serious consideration as to whether it would be best to organize it from the site or to contract for it by cartage, ship or barge; again whether to hire the ship with its crew, or to pay freightage by weight. It was less costly by water than by road and greatly advantageous when it could be floated from the quarry to the site. Both Exeter (96) and Beaulieu are examples of this method. At Exeter the main building stone came from the quarries at Beer and Salcombe 25 miles away; both it and the great blocks of Purbeck marble for the piers came by sea and up the river Exe as far as Topsham five miles from Exeter, where it was unloaded and brought to the site by road. At Beaulieu, Hampshire, built upon a tidal river, the stone was floated up, that for the exterior walling coming from Brinstead in the Isle of Wight, the interior walling from Caen in Normandy, the detailed ornament from Corfe in Dorset; the ashlar-faced walls filled in with wasters, rubble and beach boulders. Cost increased when the quarry was a distance from the site as Huddlestone was from York. In 1415 the men's wages at the quarry amounted to £9 14s., but the cost of the transport was £21 13s. 4d. Stone had to be carried from the quarry to the waterway, thence by ship or barge to York and finally by sledge to the site. In the fifteenth century Eton College had a quarry at Huddlestone; the stone at the quarry was worth 12d. a load; by the time, however, it reached Eton by cart, ship, and barge it had risen to 78d. a load.

In 1588 the conveyance of two monuments from London to Bottesford in Leicestershire entailed a journey by sea to Boston and then a transit by fifteen carts a distance of thirty miles. The journey included a broken axle; it is probable that oxen, not horses, were used for these journeys.

The building accounts for Vale Royal for the first three years 1278–80 give the total cartage of stone from quarry to site, a distance of six miles, as 34,000 loads which were paid for at the rate of 2d. or 2½d. the load, nevertheless the carters received three times more money than did the quarry men. It is evident that the roads must have been kept in good repair, for the carters averaged two journeys a day all the year round, at least sixty miles a week. These gangs were probably composed of tenants of the abbey and neighbouring farmers, or being a Royal undertaking they may have been impressed. The men, however, do not seem to have stayed for any length of time, for over 200 names of carters occur during the first thirty-six months. Although in the middle ages roads were mere trackways, certain stretches would be kept in repair as required. At Bunbury, Cheshire, the wardens' accounts for the seventeenth century mention the repair of the road to the quarry at Peckforton before carting the stone required for the rebuilding of the churchyard walls; this was evidently a usual practice and the least expensive method, for the folk who used the roads repaired them. Best of all, however, was to obtain the stone required close to the site; the excellent sandstone in large blocks used in building the fine tower at Waverton near Chester was quarried a few hundred yards from the church.

GLOSSARY OF TERMS
USED IN THE BOOK

Compiled by the Author

ABACUS.   The uppermost member of a capital immediately under the architrave.

ABUTMENT.   A pier or buttress against which an arch abuts or from which it springs.

APSIDAL.   A circular or polygonal ending to a building.

ARCH-BRACE.   A curved piece of timber extending from collar to wall-post. Any piece of timber used for supporting other timbers.

ARCUATED.   Shaped like a bow; curved in that shape or form.

ARRIS.   The sharp edge of two angles of stone or wood where they meet.

ASHLAR.   Hewn or squared stone with a smooth face to the outside wall.

ASHLAR-PIECE.   A short upright post fixed between the rafter and the inner wall-plate.

BALUSTER.   A small column or pilaster used as a support to a rail.

BARREL-VAULT.   A vault having two parallel abutments, and the same section or profile at all points, or curved as over an apse.

BATTER.   Walls having a gentle inward slope.

BATTLEMENTS.   An indented parapet used in fortifications, the solids called merlons, the openings embrasures.

BEAKHEAD.   A Norman enrichment formed of crudely shaped heads having beaks.

BILLET.   A Norman moulding formed by cutting a moulding in notches resembling short wooden billets arranged in rows.

BLIND ARCADE.   An arcade enriching a wall but unpierced.

BLIND TRACERY.   Tracery sunk in the solid not perforated.

BONDING.   Masonry effecting a union of walling either through or otherwise.

BOSS.   A carved ornament placed at the intersections of ribs in a vault either in wood or stone.

BRACE.   In carpentry any oblique piece used to brace or bind the principal timbers of a frame.

BRATTISHING.   Carved openwork in a parapet, a crest or battlement.

BRESSUMMER BEAM.   The lower beam of the front of a gallery upon which the frame of the floor is supported.

BULLNOSE MOULDING.   A rounded or obtuse moulding.

CAMBERED.   Curved slightly upwards, its object being to prevent sagging.

CAVETTO.   A concave moulding.

111

CELURE.   A canopy of honour placed over the great Rood, or an altar to enhance its dignity and stateliness.

CHAMFERED.   Formed by cutting away the arris or sharp edge of either stone or timber to any given width.

CHEVRON.   A Norman moulding of zig-zag pattern either singly used or in several numbers.

CILL.   The base of a window or base beam of a screen.

CLAMP BUTTRESS.   A buttress having flat sides of pilaster form used generally at corners.

CLERESTORY.   The third or top storey of a church containing a row of windows.

COFFERED.   A raised panelled roof the shape of the top of a chest.

COLLAR-BEAM.   A horizontal tie connecting a pair of rafters below the ridge or above the feet.

CONOIDS.   The part of a fan vault resembling a cone.

COPING.   The covering course of a wall either flat or sloping to throw off the weather.

CORBEL.   A projecting piece of stone or timber used to support wall-posts or beams.

CORBEL TABLE.   A row of corbels supporting a parapet or cornice.

COUPLE-CLOSE ROOF.   A pair of spars belonging to a roof, each independent of the next pair.

CROCKETED.   Projecting leaves, flowers, or bunches of foliage placed at regular intervals decorating an arch or gable.

CUPOLA.   A roof so called on account of its likeness to a cup turned over, a small roof in contradistinction to a dome.

CUSHION CAP.   An early Norman capital square above and circular beneath, of convex form usually crudely ornamented.

CUSPING.   Where a point is formed at the meeting of two curves with or without applied ornament.

DEMI-ANGEL.   The upper half of an angel appearing out of clouds.

DIAGONAL BUTTRESS.   A buttress constructed at the angle of a building.

DIAGONAL RIBS.   Those crossing a bay of a vault at right angles from corner to corner.

DOMICAL VAULT.   A bay of vaulting shaped like a dome.

DOUBLE OGEE.   A moulding or line formed by a combination of a round and a hollow, partly concave and partly convex, when doubled forms a design.

DOUBLE TRACERY.   A layer of tracery superimposed upon another.

DOWELLED.   Fastened together by pins either of oak or copper.

FAN VAULT.   Where all the ribs have the same curve and diverge equally in every direction.

FEATHER EDGE.   Tapered on both sides to a point and inserted into a V-shaped opening in the next plank.

FEATHERING.   A series of small arcs or foils separated by projecting points or cusps applied to the decoration of an arch.

FENESTRATION. The arrangement and proportion of windows.

FILLET. A small moulding surrounding a pier or placed horizontally or vertically dividing two mouldings.

FINIAL. The top ornament of a pinnacle or gable used generally with crockets.

FIRRED. To camber by placing firred pieces on the top of a beam, that is, to use tapering pieces to raise to the required height.

FLUSHWORK. Surface ornament. Thin carved stone slabs inserted as decoration especially in flint built churches.

FLYING BUTTRESS. A section of an arch in stone bridging from one wall to another and used as an abutment against stone vaulting.

FOILS. Feathering, producing trefoils, quatrefoils and cinquefoils in a window.

FOUR-CENTRED ARCH. The head of a window or doorway struck from four centres.

FRIEZE. A horizontal band filled in with ornament or carving.

GARGOYLE OR GURGOYLE. A projecting spout to throw off the water from the roof; often carved with grotesques.

GRAIN. The direction, arrangement and appearance of the fibres of wood or a strata of stone. The fibre which forms the substance of wood.

GRID-TRACERY. A series of narrow upright lights with cusped heads, in tracery usually divided by a transome.

GROIN. The edge formed by two intersecting vaults when left perfectly plain.

HAMMER-BEAM. The projecting sole-piece used as a cantilever to reduce the width between two walls, and for springing the arch-brace.

IMPOST. The top member of a pier or wall upon which the weight of an arch rests.

JAMBS. The sides of a window, doorway or niche.

KEYSTONE. The central or top voussoir of an arch, also where ribs of a vault meet and cross each other.

KING-POST. The centre post of a roof standing upon the tie-beam and reaching up to the ridge.

LABEL STOP. The termination often carved of a dripstone or weather moulding.

LIERNE VAULT, OR RIB. Any rib which does not rise from the springer and is not a ridge rib, but crosses from one boss to another.

MASON-STOPPED. The right-angle return of a moulding cut in the solid, in contradistinction to scribing to fit a corner.

MEDALLION. A circular or oval shape bearing a figure or symbol.

MERLON. One of the solid sections of a battlemented parapet.

MORTISE. A cavity cut into a piece of timber to receive the tenon of another piece cut to fit it.

MULLION. A slender shaft which forms the division between the lights of a window or screen.

MUNTIN. The divisions framing a piece of panelling.

NOOK-SHAFT. A pillar placed in a right angle formed by the edges of two sets of stonework used in the jambs of a doorway.

OFF-SET OR SET-OFF. The portion of a buttress which is left exposed when the part above is reduced in thickness, usually a slope.

PATERA. A small square or circular ornament spaced at regular intervals in a hollow moulding.

PENDANT. A hanging ornament from a mediaeval roof.

PILASTER STRIP. A Saxon method of building with upright stones forming a rough pilaster.

PINNACLE. A stone or timber shaft with an elongated head, crocketed at the angles and completed by a finial.

PITCH. The slope or shape of the sides of a roof to the horizon.

PLATE TRACERY. The first form of tracery of a flat surface pierced with openings in contradistinction to bar-tracery.

PLOUGH-SHARE. When a vault is skewed away from a window and does not follow its natural radius.

POLYGONAL. Many sided, having many angles.

PRINCIPAL. The frame holding up a roof and forming the point where the weight of the roof is conveyed by the purlins.

PULPITUM. A broad platformed screen separating the monks quire from the rest of the church. Usually of stone with a central doorway.

PURLIN. The horizontal cross-bars of timber from principal to principal which frame the roof holding up the rafters.

QUADRIPARTITE VAULT. Is a bay divided by diagonal ribs from corner to corner crossing at the centre and dividing the vault into four.

QUATREFOIL. A panel divided into four by feathering, either round or square.

QUEEN-POST. Two or more posts between the beam and the gable to support the principal rafters.

RABBET. A semi-groove cut longitudinally on the outer edge of a plank to receive other timber required to fit it.

RAFTER. The timbers between the principals and intermediates lying on the purlins, they support the boarding and outer roof.

RETICULATED. In tracery, a honeycomb or net pattern.

RIDGE-RIB. The stone or timber placed at the apex of the gable either in a vault or a timber roof.

RING OF AN ARCH. Each right-angled moulding of an arch forms a ring of the arch, which may be plain or moulded in sections.

ROOD. A crucifix with attendant figures of Mary and John. The Rood beam was used to support these figures.

SCANTLING. The dimensions of a piece of timber with regard to breadth and thickness but not of length.

SCRIBED. To cut a moulding in such a way as to meet it exactly at right angles or any other angle required.

SOFFIT. The underside of subordinate parts, a flat ceiling, often under a Rood loft.

SOLE-PIECE. Timbers laid across the top of a wall to form a footing for the rafters into which they are mortised.

SPANDREL. The triangular piece of stone or timber between the post and beam, used in roofs and screens often enriched with carving.

SPRINGER. The springing stone of a vault which holds the lower ends of the ribs and is bedded in the wall.

STRING COURSE. A horizontal band, whether moulded, projecting, or carved, or in any way distinguished from the rest of the walling.

STRUT. Any piece of timber used to keep apart one piece from another.

SUPERIMPOSED. To place a second layer of carving upon the first in the form of a canopy head.

TENDINOUS. Sinewy, consisting of tendons or fibres.

TENON. The projection left at the end of a piece of timber to be inserted into the socket or mortise made to receive it.

TIE-BEAM. The main beam laid across the space between the walls forming the base for the principal rafters and their support.

TIERCERON RIB. That which springs from a common source to the ridge arriving at different points but not crossing the centre.

TRACERY. The ornamental perforated filling in the head of a window, or screen or of panelling.

TRANSOM. The horizontal cross-bar to the mullions of a window or the tracery of a screen.

TRANSVERSE ARCH. An arch crossing a vault and dividing it into bays.

TREFOILED. An ornamental foliation consisting of three divisions.

TRIFORIUM, OR BLIND STOREY. The middle storey of three in which the earlier great churches were built. It was in front of the aisle roof.

TRUSS. A framed support of timber usually to uphold the roof.

TUNNEL VAULT Springs from opposite walls and presents a concave surface throughout its length.

TYMPANUM. A solid filling between loft and roof, over the head of a doorway. The space within an arch and above a lintel.

VICE. A spiral staircase from ground to roof, the steps winding round a central pillar.

VOUSSOIR. The wedge-shaped stones of which an arch is constructed.

WAGGON VAULT. See Barrel and Waggon vaults, also termed Cradle and Cylindrical.

WALL-PLATE. The timber placed along the top edge of the wall on either side of it.

WALL-POST. The upright placed against the wall tying the framework of the roof to prevent it slipping and also carrying the thrust down.

WEATHER MOULD. See dripstone label.

WEBBING. The filling in of the vault between the ribs.

INDEX TO TEXT AND ILLUSTRATIONS

Figures in *heavy type* refer to Plate References, mentioned under their
FIGURE numbers